Ancestral Motivation

By

Gumaa Francis Lodongi

Copyright © 2024 by – Gumaa Francis Lodongi – All Rights Reserved.

It is not legal to reproduce, duplicate, or transmit any part of this document in either electronic means or printed format. Recording of this publication is strictly prohibited.

Image(s) attribution:

https://www.freepik.com/

Table of Contents

About the Author i
Introduction 1
Ancient name: Akhet Khufu (Khufu's Horizon) 6
Ancient name: 300-meter Tower 13
Original name: Changcheng 17
Ancient name: The Six Grandfathers (Tȟuŋkášila Šákpe) 21
Original name: Liberty Enlightening the World 25
Wonders of The World 29
Descent With Modification 36
The Revolution of 1789 43
The Distance Between Us: Pangaea 51
The Founding Fathers of the USA 57
Madiba: Black Pimpernel 63
Jack, The Individualist mind: John F Kennedy 69
Philosophia: Love of Wisdom 77
Polymaths: The Renaissance Men 84
Changing World History 92
Epilogue 95

About the Author

Gumaa Francis Lodongi was born and raised in the beautiful Kosti, Sudan, and immigrated to beloved Canada to seek better opportunities. He wished to fulfill his dreams and goals of becoming a successful renaissance man by being an Actor, Model, Inventor, Entrepreneur, Humanitarian, Global Leader, Politician, and overall a showbiz entertainer with the inclination to break barriers, enliven matter and Humanity. He has seen the likes of many Renaissance men, such as Leonardo da Vinci, and David Michelangelo accomplish incredible success and prosperity in multiple spheres. Gumaa Francis Lodongi aspires to do a similar thing, with the exception of a plot twist.

He lived in Sudan until the age of 9 years old and for 18 years in Canada, growing and learning through cultural and traditional assimilation so that he could live the Canadian dream and spice up the diversity of Canada through his own personal upbringing to engage the human heart and re-engage the human spirit.

In this book, he aims to redefine the purpose of immigration, Inhumanity, discrimination, stereotypes, etc., by attempting to instill hope, faith, and optimism in Humanity that they may have redemptive power to live an extraordinary life, whether they're here in Canada, or somewhere else.

That is evolutionary progress, as Gumaa likes to put it. No matter the racial, national, or religious background, you can have individualistic inner and outer peace. He wishes for his Faithfuls and Admirers to keep up the Faith. May God bless you!

Introduction

Even as the modern world advances, historical structures that depict human accomplishment serve as reminders of Earth's rich history. Seven of them were considered to be "wonders": revered testaments to the contributions of historic Mediterranean and Middle Eastern ancient societies. The original selectors of these seven enigmatic sites of the early times were Hellenic travelers going through Egypt, Babylonia, and Persia. In their journey journals, works of art, and poems, they took close note of these formations.

While many of the structures constructed by the ancient societies of Africa, Europe, Asia, and the Americas were unidentified by the Hellenic peoples, these monuments are nevertheless astounding examples of ancient engineering. Beginning in the fifth century BCE, lists of wonders were compiled; the most well-known example was created by the Greek author Antipater of Sidon in the second century BCE.

The fact that, if not all, then most of these Seven Wonders have been damaged by nature, people, and time, demonstrating how transient even the greatest physical accomplishments can be. To the most extent, the element of 'wonderment' these sites possessed in earlier times has been diminished to a mere display of historical ruins or remains.

Regardless of the time, era, and condition of the site, humans have marveled at the nature of work and the intricacy applied to erect such wonder on their landscape. The question that usually pops into mind upon exploring, visiting, and pondering on these landscapes is: *why do humans feel the need to build such majestic constructions? Can humans exceed the splendor and magnificence nature has to offer?*

What if the kings and dynasts of the past were serious about becoming Gods on this Earth? What if these wonders were nothing but an exhibition of godliness by them? Perusing the pages of history, the kings of the past were worshipped as gods and considered gods — the only thing that distinguished them from God themselves was their earthly existence.

All in all, it was the unquenchable desire to be immortal, rule the world and worlds beyond it, and become the only recognizable force to exist. Gazing at the mammoth-sized pyramids, one could easily understand the claim to godliness by those kings wasn't entirely unfitting. Before the modern list of seven wonders was formed and these locations were selected, these places were commonly known as touring sites that would leave the visitor in complete awe.

People have explored and traveled far and wide to find the seven best deserving to be listed as 'the wonder of the world'. These explorers and discoverers have found out and submitted the structures they considered the best in their culture. Besides a few undisputed masterworks, not every submitted location makes it to the revered list of seven wonders.

Since universal approval and likeability for locations is forever-varying, the need to select a new and better list of seven wonders arose. The list of seven wonders we know today was determined after the Renaissance, and since then, only a few to no updates have been made. One such update was the addition of Petra, Jordan. Petra's intricately carved rock faces serve as a reminder of the prosperous and opulent civilization that once existed there. Petra is referred to in Arabic as "al-madina al ward ah," which roughly translates to "rose-colored city," a little bit more lyrical.

In the same year as Petra's inclusion in the revered list, Chichén Itzá was also named one of the wonders of the world. On the northern end of Mexico's Yucatan Peninsula, at the center of the Chichén Itza complex of Mayan ruins. Although historical records imply that Chichén Itza was in its early stages of growth between 600 and 750 A.D., archaeologists are dubious of precisely when the city's construction started.

Criteria for selection

Period:

The Official New 7 Wonders of the World encompass the entirety of human history, from the moment when Man first started leaving his mark on the planet until the year 2000 A.D.

Building quality

All monuments and constructions must be the work of humans and be in a respectable state of preservation. "Human built" denotes that individuals had to have contributed to the creation of the structure. Ruins, no matter how well-kept or visually reconstructed they were, could not be nominated for The Official New 7 Wonders since they were not in a condition of preservation where the original creators' vision could still be perceived.

Geographical scale:

There was a global call for nominations for monuments and structures from all nations and continents. However, only 21 Candidates from 21 nations made it to the final round of voting. Only one Finalist Candidate from each nation was permitted.

Value to culture and art:

Monuments and structures had to be valuable in terms of art or architecture. Future New7Wonders projects will feature unspoiled natural wonders that have not undergone human interference, as well as pure technical wonders whose primary function is the integration or usage of technology.

Relationship factor:

The monuments and structures that were nominated were all instantly recognizable.

Diversity:

Buildings and monuments reflect and honor the cultural and ethnic diversity of the world's peoples.

Ancestral motivation

A journey from the current period to that of the past and all the way to the present era. This is the true meaning of forward progress that we must make in order to make history that reverberates throughout the entire planet. Just as forgiveness forgets and forgetness forgives, the patterns of time must be conducive to our sourcing from the very early era to now. "Becoming" is simply put by former First Lady Michelle Obama, what I believe to be evidence of this incredible spanning experience.

There are ancestral factors concerning our evolutionary patterns that have empowered humanity, organisms and matter alike. We have been engineered not only from birth but as well from the trace of the first mankind to believe, serve, suffer, surrender, obey, rule, and survive. These are aspects of motivation not limited to the internally instilled graces. First and foremost, I want to talk about belief and service having forced us humanely to be inclined to prioritize such as to make a difference in the life of this cosmos starting from the reference point of family. Family is the smallest subsect, and greater than that is the neighborhood community, then the municipality, and so on and so forth. However, to serve, we must have a deep belief in service also, the potential of our realization in the matter around us, and our capacity to surmount the upcoming challenges. Belief and service are simultaneously the principles that unlock the pathways toward due inevitability.

Moreover, I'd like to point out that as modern as we are and will always be subject to the root of suffering and surrender due to previous history is that we must make amends with the necessity that is life in the intent to cope with the present issues. I like to opine just as our forefathers bore pain and agony and overcame it with such determination, we too can do the same but with greater leverage with the understanding that we lead the way and the destination shall make the way as for the fact to surrender we have to not give up but give in to the forces around us and make headway for growth sustainability. In another similar case, we shall be attuned as much as possible to Mother Earth because that is where we derive spiritual strength and nourishment.

Additionally, we should also speak of the gift of obedience, ruling, and survival. They all tie together just as the strands of fabric tie the unity. Let us obey our creator and our loving parents and the governing laws, for we shall rule and dominate our platforms of success and ascendency and ultimately prolong survivability.

In summary, thought is the ancestor to action, and action is the ancestor to the future in the same way our world is to our forefathers and us to our future generations. In order for this world to move forward and prosper and for our individual selves to be accomplished and enhanced, we ought to energize and revolutionize this world by reflecting on the past and awareness of the present and sightedness of the future.

Ancient name: Akhet Khufu (Khufu's Horizon)

The three 4th-dynasty pyramids of Giza, Arabic, Ahrāmāt Al-Jīzah, Giza, sometimes written Gizeh, were built on a rocky plateau on the west bank of the Nile River close to Al-Jzah (Giza), in northern Egypt.

The topic is included as an 'ancestral motivation', and the structure is no longer a part of the list of Seven Wonders of the World, given its fading façade.

The Giza Pyramids were designed to last forever, and they have. The massive tombs, which date back to the Old Kingdom of Egypt, were built about 4,500 years ago.

The pharaohs of Egypt believed that they would live forever as gods. They built temples for the gods and enormous pyramid tombs for themselves as preparations for the afterlife, each containing everything a monarch would require to govern and survive in the afterlife.

Around 2550 B.C., Pharaoh Khufu started construction on the first Giza pyramid. The tallest structure in Giza, His Great Pyramid, rises 481 feet (147 meters) higher than the plateau. Each of its 2.3 million stone blocks is expected to weigh 2.5 to 15 tons.

Around 2520 B.C., Pharaoh Khafre, the son of Khufu, constructed the second pyramid at Giza. The Sphinx, a strange limestone structure with a lion's body and a pharaoh's head, was also part of his necropolis. The Sphinx might watch over the entire complex of the pharaoh's tombs.

Compared to the first two Giza Pyramids, the third one is significantly smaller. It was constructed by Pharaoh Menkaure in 2490 B.C. and had a far more intricate mortuary temple.

The engineering involved

Imhotep, the first engineer ever mentioned in writing, is credited with constructing the first significant cut-stone structure, the step pyramid of the Egyptian king Djsoer in Saqqara.

Pharaohs were interred in mastabas, which were flat, rectangular buildings built above underground burial chambers prior to Imhotep. However, Imhotep was able to construct even taller structures by using stone instead of the conventional mudbrick, essentially piling six mastabas on atop one another.

Consider Imhotep, who built Djoser's pyramid using royal cubits, if you find imperial measurements to be a hassle.

A cubit is a historical unit of measurement that is regarded as being equal to the distance between the middle finger and the elbow. The cubit rods used by the ancient Egyptians to try to standardize this might range in length from 523.5 to 529.2 mm. Not quite accurate.

Although Imhotep was not the first to use stone for construction, he was certainly the first person to tackle a project of this magnitude. It is thought that Djoser's step pyramid served as a model for later pyramids, such as the colossal pyramids of Giza.

The following pyramid was constructed for King Khafre in approximately 2520 B.C. It is a bit shorter than the Great Pyramid, but because of its higher base, it is taller in elevation. Around 2490 B.C., a pharaoh by the name of Menkaure constructed the last pyramid. He built the smallest pyramid, measuring barely 215 feet (65 meters) tall.

For 3800 years, which is a significant portion of documented human history, these structures—most notably the Great Pyramid—were the tallest ever constructed. The foundation's sides completely line up with the compass's directions is another intriguing aspect of it. The North Star hadn't been in the identical place back then, and compasses weren't even a thing. To find the true north and align the foundation, Egyptian engineers would have followed the stars' motions around the sky and then divided the arcs in half.

Engineers and workmen could begin erecting the main structure when the foundation was built. The limestone used to construct the pyramids was quarried not far from the construction site. However, how did these laborers remove such big blocks from the earth? They made use of the quarry's native geology.

The density of the limestone slabs in the quarry dictated the size of each block. Naturally, these lines would split apart with little effort. Large pry bars were used to make cracks in the stone that would eventually shatter when workers dug passages down its side. This construction was really dug out of the ground and molded into place in some instances, like the huge Sphynx. One of the key ways that scientists recently were capable of deducing that ancient engineers utilized the naturally occurring limestone slabs for block width is through this construction style.

Researchers have concluded that Egyptians most likely utilized sleds that were hauled across wet sand to lessen the friction when moving the stones. By using this method, the pulling force could have been cut in half, requiring less effort for shifting the stones.

The great pyramid was constructed over the course of around 23 years, which leads many people to believe that employees could never have finished the project without outside assistance. However, when you dissect the arithmetic, you can see that it is feasible.

More than 900 kilometers (560 miles) to the south, in Aswan, the granite stones for the pyramid were shipped. The largest granite stone was installed in the ceilings of the "King's chamber" and the "relieving chambers", weighing up to 25-80 tons. By pounding grooves into the faces of natural stone, inserting wooden wedges, and then soaking these in water, the ancient Egyptians carved stone into rough blocks. The wedges grew as the water became saturated and broke off manageable portions. After being carved, the blocks were transported to the pyramid by boat across the Nile River.

What about the construction crew who built the pyramids? Huge, intricate towns that might have housed thousands of qualified staff and entire families have been discovered by Egyptologists everywhere around the sites of the pyramids. The notion that slaves were employed in the building of the structures has been disproven by recent studies. Graffiti by workers discovered at Giza suggests that haulers were organized into 40-man groups called zau (plural za), each of which had a "Overseer of Ten" and was made up of four sub-units. There is a lot of evidence to suggest that Egyptian society held construction workers and architects in high regard.

The King's, Queen's, and Subterranean Chambers, the Grand Gallery, as well as a number of shafts and corridors, make up the internal structure. The original entrance and a forced route, which converge at a confluence, are the two entrances to the pyramid. One path leads down to the Subterranean Chamber from there, and the other leads up to the Grand Gallery.

Tracing back wondrous history

The Great Pyramid was once thought to have been built exclusively by Khufu, placing its construction during his reign. So, determining the pyramid's age required determining Khufu's and the 4th dynasty's ages. This strategy focuses on the relative timing and synchronicity of events.

Actual date ranges are determined from a network of interconnected facts based on the succession lines deduced from texts and old king lists. The kingship durations from Khufu to estimated points in the distant past are summarized and supported by information from ancestry, astronomy, and other sources. The historical timeline of Egypt is, therefore, essentially a political timeline, making it distinct from different forms of archaeological proof.

Mantheo's chronology

The foundation for the contemporary chronology of Egyptian history is made up of a number of literary sources. The writings of Manetho (Ma-Net-Ho) are the most significant of all. He was an Egyptian priest who served at the Temple of Sebennytos in the Delta and flourished between 305-285 BC under the rule of Ptolemy I and Ptolemy II. He was familiar with Greek and Egyptian hieroglyphs and, as a priest, had access to primary sources, including historical documents and king lists. Additionally, he was able to make inferences from his own firsthand knowledge of religious rituals, festivals, and customs. He is credited with eight works; the Aegyptiaca

(History of Egypt), his most significant, was composed during the rule of Ptolemy II.

Predictions of the durations of each monarch's reign are given in Manetho's history, and he also includes fables about the kings, clearly drawing on both the official records and unofficial material. Since it was obviously constructed using the author's firsthand knowledge of the ancient records, if this history had remained complete, it would have made for the best chronological record of Egyptian history that is currently available. Manetho's writings, however, have yet to be fully discovered; instead, they have only been preserved in edited excerpts in the works of the Jewish historian Flavius Josephus (about 70 AD), whose writings were still regarded in the era of the Renaissance as a foundational resource for researching ancient Egypt.

The history of Manetho also had a significant impact on biblical studies. With reference to the timeline of the Exodus from Egypt during Moses and the timeline of the after-flood in Noah's years, his extensive chronological past offered a possible grounds for determining the times for biblical events.

Chronology in the countries outside of Egypt, in particular in Canaan and Mesopotamia, depended on chronological ties to events inside of Egypt. Manetho had an early effect on the advancement of the chronology of kingdoms outside Egypt.

It has occasionally been feasible to confirm or disprove Manetho's claims using data from archaeological discoveries and other historical writings. Manetho's chronology continues to serve as the foundation for the present, acknowledged list of kings and dynasties despite its flaws and shortcomings. However, by making it possible for researchers to understand the ancient texts, Champollion's first discovery and subsequent research revolutionized the exploration of Egyptian history. This gave Egyptologists access to information on Egyptian history and the reigns that were recorded in many known inscriptions titled "king's list".

The building of the Great Pyramid included extensive use of mortar. Ashes from fires, organic substances that were likely to be removed, and radiocarbon-dated material were all incorporated into the mortar during the mixing process. In order to ensure that the mortar was unquestionably part of the original construction and was not added afterward, 46 samples of it were collected in 1984 and 1995. From 2871–2604 BC, the results were calibrated.

The historically derived chronology was found to be roughly accurate by the recently developed radiocarbon dating technique. Due to wider margins of error, calibration uncertainties, and the issue of intrinsic age (the period between growth and eventual usage) in plant substances, particularly wood, it is still not a fully acknowledged technology. Furthermore, it has been proposed that construction dates and astronomical alignments are related.

Flinders Petrie was a British Egyptologist who worked meticulously to study the Giza necropolis and dig the Great Pyramid in the late 19th and early 20th centuries. The Great Pyramid at Giza wasn't ever misplaced or concealed; thus, it could never be found or found again. Throughout the period of the pyramids' construction, the Giza region has been constantly inhabited, unlike numerous other historical sites in Egypt and worldwide.

Ancient name: 300-meter Tower

French architect Gustave Eiffel, whose business specialized in creating metal frames and constructions, constructed the Eiffel Tower between 1887 and 1889.

The Eiffel Tower was constructed to serve as one of the centerpieces of the 1889 Paris World's Fair. The massive iron and steel structures that represented the era's greatest industrial achievement were the highlight of that year's World's Fair, which filled the whole Champ de Mars in Paris. On May 15, 1889, the day of the World's Fair, The Tower was unveiled to the public.

The Eiffel Tower became one of the most well-known attractions in Paris very fast due to its height and distinctive silhouette soaring above the cityscape. The fate of the Eiffel Tower is tightly entwined with that of Paris, the nation's capital and owner.

The Eiffel Tower has served as Paris' and, ultimately, France's powerful and recognizable symbol for 130 years. When it was initially constructed for the 1889 World's Fair, it dazzled everyone with its size and audacious design, and it stood for French innovation and technical prowess.

It took an unprecedented 2 years, 2 months, and 5 days to construct the Eiffel Tower between the end of January 1887 and March 31, 1889. The Tower's speedy construction was an unprecedented feat at the time, in addition to its technical and architectural expertise.

The top, second level, and first floor of the Tower are all accessible to the general public. The peak and the second floor both have two levels—a covered lower level and an uncovered level above. The first two levels are accessible to guests via elevator or stairs. The only way to get from the second floor to the top is by elevator.

The weight of the Eiffel Tower is roughly 10,100 tons. While the paint used to preserve the building "only" weighs 60 tons, the metal framework itself weighs 7,300 tons!

The enormous iron structure will swing during a storm while being wind-resistant. The gigantic Tower may also be moved by the intense radiation of the sun, which causes iron expansion and cause the Tower to enlarge by roughly six inches throughout warmer months. 72 of the scientists and engineers who worked in France throughout the 19th century also had their names inscribed on the Eiffel Tower. Following a restoration effort, the engraved tributes were once again made visible. Visitors with keen eyes may again see inscriptions like Foucault, Dumas, and Perrier etched into the iron.

Lighting was first added to the Tower in 1985 with the installation of 336 yellow-orange bulbs, but it wasn't until New Year's Eve 1999—to usher in the new millennium—that the 20,000-bulb glittering light show made its debut.

The construction schedule

Initiation of construction	26th January 1887
Beginning of the pillars' mounting	1st July 1887
First-floor completion	1st April 1888
Second-floor completion	14th August 1888
Top and assembly completion	31st March 1889

The license rights associated with the standard for the skyscraper's construction had been predetermined to expire after 20 years, at which point the tower would be demolished when the concept was first conceived. However, during the Universal Exposition, the Tower saw two million visitors. After achieving such astounding success, the structure came to represent the might of the French industry. The Tower enjoyed the same level of success at the 1900 International Exposition. The architect, Gustave Eiffel, went to considerable lengths to demonstrate the Tower's scientific value in an effort to stop its destruction.

Astronomical and physiological research was done, but in the end, the Tower's use as a radio antenna tower — first for military communications, then for ongoing radiotelegraphy communications — would be what really saved it. In fact, the Tower served a variety of functions during the First World War. The history of France includes the Eiffel Tower.

About 7 million people climb the Tower each year. Due to its widespread success, numerous nations have built replicas of the Tower that are almost exact replicas of the original.

ORIGINAL NAME: CHANGCHENG

The Great Wall of China, also known as Wanli Changcheng or Wan-li Ch'ang-ch'eng ("10,000-Li Long Wall"), is a massive fortification that was built in ancient China. It was one of the biggest architectural undertakings ever.

Chinese authorities launched wall-building initiatives for millennia to defend the country from nomadic invaders. Around Shandong, a part of one such ancient wall that is still standing is made of the hard-packed soil known as "rammed earth," and it is thought to be 2,500 years old. Such walls protected the borders for many years throughout the Warring States Period when China was united into one country.

China was unified by Qin Shi Huang, often known as the First Emperor, in 220 BCE. He oversaw the integration of the current walls into a single structure. The state of Chu began constructing a permanent defense system around the 7th century BCE. This barrier, also known as the "Square Wall," was located in the northern region of the kingdom's capital province.

The Hexi ("West of the [Yellow] River") and Henan ("South of the River") walls were two safeguards in the Wei state. Defense from the Qin state and western nomads, the Hexi Wall was built. In an effort to protect the land from attacks by northern factions like the Donghu, Linhu, and Loufan and from incursions by the Qi state in the south, the Yan state constructed two distinct defensive lines: the Northern Wall and the Yishui Wall.

The wall was constructed primarily of wood and rammed dirt that period across the Yellow Sea. Emperor after emperor built on and strengthened the wall, frequently in an effort to stave off northern invaders. The wall was made of brick in certain areas. Granite, as well as marble slabs from quarries, were employed in other places. As construction methods improved, the wall was continually updated.

The Ming Dynasty was started by Zhu Yuanzhang, who is renowned for his accomplishments in the pottery and painting arts. Watchtowers and platforms were added to the wall by the Ming emperors. The majority of popular pictures of the wall depict its stone construction during the Ming era. The wall runs from 4,000 to 5,500 kilometers (2,500 and 3,400 miles), depending on how it is calculated.

The Manchu rulers expanded Chinese power into Inner Mongolia during the 17th century, which diminished the wall's defensive value. Its significance as a representation of Chinese cultural identity and heritage hasn't diminished, either.

The Great Wall also aided in the expansion of the Silk Road trade route and the exploitation of agricultural land in the north and western regions of China. The Great Wall was used for protection as well as for centralized management of trade and transportation.

The majority of the Great Wall as it exists now was constructed under the Hongzhi emperor's (1487–1505) rule. This section of the wall, which began west of Juyong Pass, was divided into south and north paths, known alternately as the Inner and Outer walls. There were numerous purposeful "passes" (i.e., forts) and gates along the wall. The three nearest to the Ming capital Beijing were the Juyong, Daoma, and Zijing passes. They were collectively known as the Three Inner Passes. The Three Outer Passes, also known as Yanmen, Ningwu, and Piantou, were located further west. There were three main parts to the Great Wall: passages, signal towers (beacons), and walls.

The Great Wall of China has been constructed in portions that total 21,196 kilometers (13,171 miles) in length, including overlapped sections that were restored. The longest and best-preserved part of the wall was built during the Ming dynasty and is around 8,850 kilometers (5,499 miles) long.

Due to weather exposure and socioeconomic changes throughout history, much of its original beauty has been compromised. After the People's Republic of China was established, steps were taken to safeguard it. The Great Wall was recognized as a significant historical site with State protection in 1961. Mostly the parts at Badaling, Shanhaiguan Pass, and Jiayuguan Pass have undergone maintenance and repairs.

The Great Wall was added to the UNESCO (United Nations Educational, Scientific, and Cultural Organization) List of World Heritages in 1987.

Ancient name: The Six Grandfathers (Tȟuŋkášila Šákpe)

Even before Mount Rushmore National Memorial was finished 79 years ago on October 31, 1941, it was controversial because it was constructed on sacred Native American ground and was sculpted by a man with affiliations to the Ku Klux Klan.

With 60-foot-tall portraits etched into a South Dakota granite, Mount Rushmore honors four US presidents: George Washington, Thomas Jefferson, Theodore Roosevelt, and Abraham Lincoln. The monument has sparked opposition throughout the years due to its placement on Native American territory and discussions about if another commander-in-chief is worthy of a place on the mountain.

The Native Americans of the Great Plains used it as a place of worship and prayer before it was recognized as Mount Rushmore. Another important factor was the mountain's position within the Black Hills. Euro-American settlers started moving towards the Black Hills in the late 1800s, sparking a conflict with the local populace. The Treaty of Fort Laramie, which the U.S. government entered in 1868, granted the Lakota the exclusive possession of the Black Hills. However, gold was found in the area within a decade, and the U.S. breached the pact and seized the territory in 1877.

A historian who worked at the South Dakota State Historical Society named Doane Robinson thought the state needed to do more to draw tourists. Robinson started an initiative in 1924 to develop South Dakota's own mountain men. He got in touch with Gutzon Borglum, the Stone Mountain artist who would turn the granite mountainside into the monument it is today. Borglum had achieved acclaim for his sculptures but was sacked after getting affiliated with the Ku Klux Klan. However, he eventually consented to sculpt the presidents in his own unique method after a few months. Borglum fought with the US government over Mount Rushmore's finances and authority for the following 16 years.

When Borglum's health started to decline, he was still perfecting those skulls. On March 6, 1941, he passed away, leaving his son Lincoln to carry on his job. However, there was only so much of the mountain that could be carved; for instance, the condition of the stone prevented finishing Jefferson's hand; what's more, money had run out. The undertaking was deemed complete on October 31, 1941.

While some have advocated for Mount Rushmore's expansion, others have called for its destruction. Some tribe officials and those who support them have asked for the memorial's removal as the United States continues to address the Confederate statues along with other reminders of its racist history.

How big are the faces?

George Washington's nose is 21 feet (6.4 m) tall, and his head is 60 feet (18.3 m) tall. Abraham Lincoln's head is significantly taller, while Theodore Roosevelt's is a little smaller.

The width of each eye on Mount Rushmore is roughly 11 feet (3.4 meters). The width of each mouth is roughly 18 feet (5.5 m). The sculpture is expected to erode at a rate of one inch per 10,000 years. 5,725 feet above sea level is where Mount Rushmore's peak is located.

The US Constitution, the Declaration of Independence, the Bill of Rights, a biography of Borglum, and brief summaries of each of the presidents shown on the monument are currently concealed behind a 1,200-pound granite block and nestled into a wooden box.

The memorial's rocks are being steadily eroded by the effects of wind and weather. Granite is incredibly resilient, though. Only 1/10 inch per thousand years has been calculated as the rate of corrosion on the granite faces.

The granite blocks in the artwork were recognized and sorted using a technique called key block analysis. The faces of George Washington, Abraham Lincoln, and Theodore Roosevelt contain four blocks that have been identified as potential key blocks. It is thought that if one of these three potential key blocks moved, it would allow other granite blocks to follow suit.

The outdated silicone sealant was started being removed by National Park Service employees and replaced. The high temperature and moisture changes that take place on Mount Rushmore can be better tolerated by modern sealants. The silicone is covered in granite dust to conceal it after application, much like Borglum had done.

Original name: Liberty Enlightening the World

The copper monument was being built as a present to America by French sculptor Frédéric Auguste Bartholdi and his team, who also included Gustave Eiffel, the man behind the creation of the famed Eiffel Tower. Specifically, it was meant to be a kind gesture after the American Civil War.

A few female figures, notably a goddess of Rome named Libertas and an Arab woman from Bartholdi's earlier design for an Egyptian statue, served as inspiration for the Statue of Liberty. The sculptor's mother, Charlotte, also served as the inspiration for the statue's face. Libertas stood for both individual and societal freedom and independence. Bartholdi picked Libertas as the model for the bronze Statue of Liberty since she was frequently shown as a robed woman.

A statue of liberty for the nation of America was suggested in 1865 by Edouard de Laboulaye, a French political thinker and anti-slavery fighter. This memorial would celebrate the 100th anniversary of American independence as well as the country's connection with France.

The French chose to ship the sculpture in 350 separate pieces because of its huge New York location. As soon as it arrived in 1884 on Bedloe Island, now known as Liberty Island, it was put together and set atop a pedestal that the Americans had first constructed. Under Bartholdi's leadership, work on the Statue's construction in France started in 1876. The torch-holding arm was finished in 1876 and displayed at the Philadelphia Centennial Exposition. Completed in 1878, the head and shoulders were on display at the Paris Universal Exposition. Between 1881 and 1884, the statue's whole construction and assembly took place in Paris. The pedestal's American building work started in 1884 as well.

The statue was disassembled and transported to the United States on the French Navy ship Isère after being handed to Levi P Morton, the U.S. ambassador to France, on July 4, 1884, in Paris. On June 17, 1885, the statue sailed to New York Harbor for a lot of celebration. Sadly, the statue's pedestal was not yet finished, and the entire edifice was not put back together on Bedloe's Island until 1886.

Lady Liberty's pedestal, which is designed like a star, is famous, although it wasn't made for her. On the ruins of Fort Wood, that was constructed between 1808 and 1811, the pedestal is located. Fort Wood, which was created to defend the city from British invasion, was given that name in honor of an Army engineer who perished in the War of 1812. The National Park Service now owns the fort's remnants, which were formerly an army station until 1937.

It is hardly surprising considering Lady Liberty weighs a massive 225 tons and has an elevation comparable to the enormous size of this pedestal.

The Statue of Liberty is 305 feet and 1 inch tall from its foundation to the tip of the flame. Visitors must climb 354 stairs, or 20 stories, to reach the crown, with the statue's 879 shoe size standing at roughly the halfway mark. Although the iconic Statue of Liberty is an American landmark, the idea of freedom it represents is international. This is symbolized by the seven continents and the seven seas on its crown.

The torch is a representation of illumination. It is intended to illuminate the route to freedom and direct us toward the direction of justice and liberty. There was even a suggestion that the sculpture could really light the path for sailors entering New York Harbor at one point.

With a 23-foot-long block of copper in its left hand, the statue's left hand is seated by her side. The words "July 4, 1776" are written in Roman numerals on what is essentially a tablet. Due to its connection to the United States' Declaration of Independence, Bartholdi decided on this day as the anniversary of American independence. He held the American struggle for freedom and independence, along with the U.S. Constitution, in the highest regard. The tablet is a representation of a book of law. The shape is more like a keystone than a square.

There are chains and a broken shackle around Lady Liberty's feet. The depiction of Diana as a goddess liberated from captivity and servitude closely reflects the country's recent legalization of the practice at the time of her inauguration. Her clothes partially conceal the shackles, making it practically difficult to see them from the ground.

The Sonnet

Money-raising activities were held all throughout the city as the pedestal's funding campaign got underway in the US. Emma Lazarus was requested to help by providing a unique piece of art that would be sold at auction. "The New Colossus" is the sonnet that was created; as a result, paying homage to the statue's meaning as a lighthouse for hope. Lady Liberty has earned the moniker "Mother of Exiles" from Lazarus.

>Not like the brazen giant of Greek fame,
>With conquering limbs astride from land to land;
>Here at our sea-washed, sunset gates shall stand
>A mighty woman with a torch, whose flame
>Is the imprisoned lightning, and her name
>Mother of Exiles. From her beacon-hand
>Glows world-wide welcome; her mild eyes command
>The air-bridged harbor that twin cities frame.
>"Keep, ancient lands, your storied pomp!" cries she
>With silent lips. "Give me your tired, your poor,
>Your huddled masses yearning to breathe free,
>The wretched refuse of your teeming shore.
>Send these, the homeless, tempest-tost to me,
>I lift my lamp beside the golden door!"

Emma Lazarus
November 2, 1883

WONDERS OF THE WORLD

To document the most breathtaking natural features and man-made monuments in the world, multiple lists of the marvels of the world were prepared from antiquity to the present.

The Seven Wonders of the Ancient World is the earliest list of its kind known to exist.

It lists the most amazing man-made structures from classical antiquity. Because it was based on travel guides widely used by Hellenic tourists, it only includes structures found in the ancient regions of the Near East and along the Mediterranean coast. Given that there were five known planets in ancient times, plus the Sun and Moon, the number seven was chosen as the Greeks thought it symbolized abundance and perfectionThe Swiss charity 7 Wonders launched the initiative to choose the next seven wonders of the world in 2000. These seven were named as the winners in 2007, and the entire ranking was made available. Since the first "Seven Wonders of the World" were organized by Philo of Byzantium in 250 B.C., merely mentioning the "Seven Wonders" is no longer obvious enough for a reader to understand the framework.

Some authors imitated the classical list in the 19th and early 20th centuries by compiling their own lists under titles like "Wonders of the Middle Ages," "Seven Wonders of the Middle Ages," "Seven Wonders of the Medieval Mind," and "Architectural Marvels of the Middle Ages."

New Wonders of The World

1. Roman Colosseum

The Flavian Amphitheatre, often known as the Colosseum or Coliseum, was built in Rome and opened in AD 80 by Titus, the son of Vespasian, for one hundred days of games that featured gladiatorial combat and animal competitions. One of the Seven Wonders of the World, it. It is one of the most popular tourist attractions even though two-thirds of the actual building have been ruined over time. Given that the Romans built this magnificent structure about 2,000 years ago, it is astonishing that it is still standing today. The Colosseum continues to be the only permanent, immovable symbol of Rome's past despite the city's tremendous episodes of development over time.

Unsurprisingly, a significant amount of labor was required to build such a substantial and intricate public monument. Along with teams of skilled builders, painters, and designers who labored for the Roman Emperor, around 100,000 slaves brought over from the Jewish war were used for the physically demanding manual labor. The Colosseum culminated in completion six years after construction started, in 79 AD.

2. Máximo Picchu

Hiram Bingham "found" Machu Picchu, an Incan site in Peru, in 1911.One of the Seven Wonders of the World, it. It is a short distance from Cuzco. Vilcabamba was what he believed it to be, a secret Incan stronghold utilized throughout the 16th-century struggle against Spanish dominance. It is among the few known large pre-Columbian remains that had been discovered virtually intact.

The Temple of the Sun, erected on a prominent vantage point to commemorate the Incan sun god Inti, is one of the most significant structures on the property. The Incas probably performed a number of rites, sacrifices, and celebrations in this temple in reverence of the sun deity. Machu Picchu's whole complex spans 5 km and has 150 separate structures. These include water fountains, residences, plazas, temples, sanctuaries, bathhouses, and mausoleums. The Temple of the Sun, the Temple of the Three Windows, and Inti Watana, a carved stone sundial or calendar, are among the attractions.

Granite from nearby quarries was used to build the holy citadel of Machu Picchu by tens of thousands of people. They used a remarkable variety of drystone techniques to build the complete structure, fitting the irregularly shaped stone pieces snugly together like jigsaw puzzle pieces. Through this method, the Incas were able to construct buildings that were indestructible and had stood for over 500 years.

3. Petra

Southern Jordan has a fascinating historic town called Petra. Due to its color, it is commonly referred called Raqmu or Rose City. One of the Seven Wonders of the World, Petra is believed to have been built as a trading hub by the Nabataean, an indigenous Arab clan who lived in the region that is now southwest Jordan. Petra was a hub of trade in the region at the time because of its location, lying roughly 150 miles in the southern part of Jerusalem and Amman, the main city of Jordan, and about halfway to Damascus, Syria, and the Red Sea.

The city had been lost for many years, but it was found again in 1812, leading historians to refer to it as the "Lost City of Petra." We take a look at a few details on this amazing ancient archaeological marvel, whose history goes all the way back to the fourth century BCE. Red, white, and pink-hued sandstone from a nearby quarry is used to construct half of Petra and carve the other half. Even the name of the city is taken from the rocks of which it is composed: the Greek word "petros."

Amazingly, just 15% of Petra was successfully explored and made accessible to visitors so far. The remainder of the metropolis, which historians estimate to be 100 square miles in size and four times the size of Manhattan, is still hidden behind piles of debris and has not yet been discovered. Amazingly, more than 30,000 individuals formerly called this sizable area home.

4. Taj Mahal

One of the finest examples of the work of Mughal architecture is the marble mausoleum complex known as the Taj Mahal in Agra, India. It was constructed by Shah Jahan (who ruled between 1628–58) in honor of Mumtaz Maal, dubbed "Chosen One of the Palace," who died in 1631 while delivering their fourteenth child. The Taj Mahal building is said to have been carried out by 20,000 artisans under the supervision of a team of skilled architects of the time.

The dazzling white marble used to construct Mumtaz Mahal's tomb symbolizes the emperor's unwavering loyalty to his cherished bride. 1632 saw the start of construction, which lasted until 1648. In 1653, the emperor Shah Jahan constructed several components, such as a mosque, guesthouse, and southern entryway.

The building and grounds were created by Indian architect Ustad-Ahmad Lahori. He went to tremendous pains to make the Mughal era an icon.

The Taj Mahal is said to have required 20,000 devoted workers to complete in its entirety. Together, they produced a masterwork that has stood the test of time exceptionally well. The supplies they used came from all around Asia and India, often being transported by elephants. The Taj Mahal was built by this enormous team over the course of 22 years and at a cost of 32 million rupees (about $827 million USD).

5. Christ the Redeemer Statue

The Christ, the Redeemer monument, sometimes called Cristo Redentor, is an Art Deco-style monument of Jesus that is located on Mount Corcovado in Rio de Janeiro. The 130-foot statue, which is built of hardened concrete and soapstone, was designed by Heitor da Silva Costa. About $250,000 went into its construction, most of which came from donations. It is located on the highest point of Corcovado Mountain within Tijuca Forest National Park and weighs 635 tonnes. It offers vistas of Rio de Janeiro.

The group considered various options before settling on one from the engineer Heitor da Silva Costa and the artist Carlos Oswald, whose concept was to depict Christ with his arms extended, carrying a cross in one hand while grasping a big sphere in the other.

Paul Landowski, a well-known French-Polish sculptor, was chosen by Da Silva in 1923 to create the erect form for the sculpture of Christ the Redeemer. Landowski suggests depicting Christ with his hands empty and his palms open, seemingly bewildered at the crucifixion cross, building on Da Silva's original idea of him with his arms open.

The internal structure of the sculpture and the enlargement of the body were conceptualized by French engineer Albert Caquot during the construction stage of the finished statue of Christ the Redeemer. Last but not least, the statue's head and face were sculpted by Romanian artist Gheorghe Leonida. He was the one who gave the image of Christ its final breath, and together, this extremely talented group produced a contemporary masterpiece.

6. Greater China Wall

The Great Wall of China is a construction feat that is thought to be about 5,500 miles (8,850 km) long; nevertheless, the Chinese assert that it is truly 13,170 miles (21,200 km) long. Beginning in the 7th century BCE, the Great Wall was constructed over the period of two millennia. At the time, the remarkable organization's objectives included border control, levies on Silk Road trade, supervision of commerce and migration, and defense.

7. Chichen Itzá

Chichen Itza is a Mayan metropolis located in Mexico. The Yucatán Peninsula, where it is situated, experienced immense wealth during the ninth and tenth centuries A.D. It is also believed that Chichen Itza is one of the mythical great cities, or Tollans, described in later Mesoamerican literature. The Maya Civilization left behind a number of religious buildings amid the city's ruins, including the Temple of Kukulkán, with 365 stairs, each for every single day following the Haab solar calendar.

This historic location provides an intriguing look into the tens of thousands of Mayans who once called this place home and gives a wealth of information about ancient civilizations.

Chichen Itza gets its name from both the location and the inhabitants who built it. Chichen refers to the "mouth of the well," a reference to the Xtoloc Cenote that supplied the city with a reliable source of water. The Itzaes, often known as "water witches," who first inhabited the region in or about the fifth century CE, are referenced in the term "Itza." Chichen Itza's main city has a space of around 5 square kilometers, and beyond it are the remnants of smaller residential structures. A number of monuments and monasteries may be found in the city's core, each with an intriguing historical value.

Honorable Mention: Sigiriya

A century-old stone fortress Sigiriya (The Lion Rock), which was used by a monarch of Sri Lanka as a location to construct his royal residence and escape from his brother's raids, is frequently regarded as the eighth wonder. The stronghold, which is located in Sri Lanka's central Matale District, is encircled on all sides by the ruins of a vast network of gardens and reservoirs. These gardens are thought to be among the earliest landscaped ones in existence.

The popularity of the Lion Mountain seems attributable to the tale of Kashyapa, who founded his capital here despite the fact that the rock actually was already frequented in the third century. The monarch, a son of Dhatusena, established his rule by planning his own father's murder and driving out his brother. Up until the 14th century, Sigiriya became a Buddhist monastery after the death of the king. Majestic frescoes from the location served as inspiration for an artistic language that was used for over a century.

Descent With Modification

Where the world is brimming with man-made wonders, man and its origins remain a miracle not yet fully explored. Some say men have changed over time, termed as evolution, from ape-like beings to the current human form. Darwinism is one such theory proposing the idea of human origin.

All scientific ideas about the diversity of species through mutation and selection that emerged after Darwin's book The Origin of Species in 1859 are collectively referred to as Darwinism. The term "Darwinism" typically encompasses every idea of evolution after Darwin. The term became commonplace every time the idea of the principle of natural selection and its traits were talked about. This is true even though there are many significant differences between Darwin's view of evolution and later theories. The theory of explaining cultural features, cultural behavior, and advances in humankind by the processes proposed by Darwin is frequently referred to as "Darwinism," which has a broader definition.

According to this theory, the 'natural selection' of certain living things over others is the true driving force behind change. This occurs when more living things are born compared to those who can survive and thrive, a few of which possess traits that aid them in the ensuing 'struggle for existence,' and these are then weeded out or chosen to serve as breeding ones for all generations to come.

Change is occurring, and it is moving in the direction of "adaptive" excellence, which is to say that creatures are developing traits to help them survive and procreate. These conclusions, which hold true for all species, including humans, have had a significant impact on how we have since thought about science, philosophy, and religion.

So how are we to describe and classify "Darwinism" or a "Darwinian," the latter of which refers to someone who adopts the philosophy in order to connect together threads from the past and the present? Darwinism unmistakably binds one to the reality of evolution. Some Darwinists believe that their stance also necessitates acceptance of some form of philosophical materialism, asserting that any sort of supernatural belief is erroneous or implausible. Even though this is undeniable that one need not be a Darwinian to agree with a tree of life, Darwinism itself undoubtedly is based on some sort of tree of life when it comes to evolution as a path.

Natural selection is the theory behind evolution put forth by Charles Darwin. Given the scarcity of resources in nature, animals with heritable features that promote both fertility and survival will typically produce more offspring versus their contemporaries, leading to an increase in the frequency of such traits across successive generations.

Populations change throughout time through natural selection, becoming increasingly adapted to their surroundings. Natural selection is reliant upon the environment and necessitates the presence of heritable variation within a population.

Changing numbers and kinds of creatures are at the heart of biological evolution. The British naturalist Charles Darwin is most likely the first individual that comes to mind today when we discuss evolution. Charles Darwin initially appears to be an improbable revolutionary. He appeared to be idle and aimless, according to his father, as a meek and modest child of a prosperous British household. But Darwin showed a keen curiosity in nature even as a young child. He was afterward given the opportunity to work as a volunteer naturalist on the HMS Beagle, which was a navy ship setting off on an exploration voyage around the world while pursuing botany at Cambridge University. Over the course of almost five years at sea, the Beagle explored the South American coast and made stops in Australia and, most notably, the Galapagos Islands.

Darwin discovered that different but related species of finches lived on neighboring islands in the Galápagos. Additionally, he pointed out that each species of finch was appropriate for its habitat and function. In particular, species that consumed big seeds typically had big, thick beaks, but species that consumed insects typically had thin, pointy beaks. Finally, he noted that while the finches (and other creatures) seen on the Galápagos Islands were distinct when compared to those located someplace else in the world, they were related to species on the nearby Ecuadorian mainland.

On his journey, Darwin did not discover all of this. In fact, until he later exhibited his specimens to an expert ornithologist (bird biologist), he was unaware that all finches were related but unique species. Darwin claimed that all organisms share a common ancestry, that they evolve through time, and that new species develop from existing ones. According to this theory, each species has a distinct set of genetic variations inherited from the common ancestral lineage that has developed gradually over extremely long time periods. A multi-level "tree" connecting all living things is created through periodic branching events, which occur when diverse species are born and evolved from that shared lineage.

Darwin did more than only suggest that organisms evolved, which is important. Natural selection was the process Darwin also suggested for evolution. This method explained how populations might develop (undergo derivation with change) so that they could become more suited to their habitats through time. It was elegant and reasonable.

Natural selection does not prefer characteristics that are better in some fundamental way. Instead, it rewards characteristics that, in that environment, will enable a creature to survive and reproduce better than its predecessors. In some environments, traits that are advantageous can really be harmful. Heritable variation serves as the initial source of variation for natural selection. Evidently has to be a variable (differences between individuals) for a feature for evolution to take place on it. Additionally, the variations must be inherited, as indicated by the DNA of the organisms.

Darwin's theory that existing species, including humans, had evolved over time as a result of random and continual change appeared to be in direct conflict with the view that all living things had been created "according to their kind" by God, as stated in biblical scriptures. The preeminent scientific view of the origins and development of life stated that species had no variability and never changed until Darwin. This idea, also referred to as "special creationism," is in line with the Bible's narrative of God creating fish, birds, and mammals without any hint of later modification.

The idea that man had a unique, God-given role in the natural order, which is fundamental to Christianity and a variety of faiths, also seemed to be in conflict with Darwinian Theory. Rather, supporters of evolution cited physical characteristics of humans, such as the remains of a tailbone, that demonstrate a shared ancestry with other animals.

The DNA and genes within the gametes—the sperm or egg cells that help parents transfer their genetic makeup to their offspring—cause physiological and psychological modifications that enable natural selection. Mutations are the name given to such alterations. Unexpected defects in gene replication or repair, as well as radiation or chemical damage, can result in mutations. Rarely, a mutation may prove advantageous to the organism. Mutations are typically either detrimental or neutral. That way, it will spread across the population and become more common in the following generation.

Natural selection directs evolution in this way, maintaining and accumulating advantageous mutations while eliminating harmful ones. While mutations are random, their selection is not random.

One may argue that a species continuously adjusts to its surroundings as it evolves over time. The characteristics of people who do not live enough years for procreation are lost to the species. As natural selection takes place within the species, noticeable variations (in size, color, or other features) may manifest over time. The species will have changed from its original state after hundreds of generations, but no new evolutionary branches will have formed.

After many generations, inhabitants of one population may develop adaptations that may prevent them from successfully mating with individuals from other populations. These adaptations could be behavioral, like the evolution of mating calls, or physical, such as changes in size, coloring, or body chemistry. The remote populations may eventually diverge to such a degree that each becomes a distinct species.

Darwin also observed trends in the clustering of similarly related organisms throughout time. The fossil record has numerous instances of species with similar appearances coexisting in a single layer or between strata of rock. Natural selection's effects could also be seen in growing embryos, where the structures of more primitive animals mirrored those of higher vertebrates during the early stages of development.

Generally speaking, the closer one organism's evolutionary relationship is to another, the more qualities both organisms have in common.

Honorable mention: Alfred Wallace

Wallace traversed the globe, examining and gathering samples of many species, much like Charles Darwin. During his travels, he gathered countless samples of plants, birds, insects, and other creatures. He also visited Brazil and a number of the Malay Archipelago islands that today make up Indonesia and the Philippines. Wallace opted to move back to England after spending a four-year stint in Brazil due to health reasons. However, the ship met an accident and perished in the Atlantic 26 days into their return trip. All of Wallace's notes and materials were lost at sea, and his team and the ship's crew drifted at sea for ten days before being rescued by a passing ship. Having undergone this failure, Wallace embarked on a further journey to Southeast Asia in 1854 to gather more samples.

He then fell ill once more in 1858 in Southeast Asia. He was feverish and had hallucinations, but once the fever subsided, he realized the solution: species change as a result of environmental adaptation! Wallace was aware that Darwin was engaged in related research. He wrote Darwin a letter in 1858 detailing his views on evolution. They worked together on a scientific publication where they presented their arguments for evolution and natural selection.

Wallace traveled to Southeast Asia for eight years to conduct research and gather biological samples. He collected about 125,000 samples at that time. His studies on the geographical spread of creatures gave his views on evolution crucial support and inspired him to separate animal groupings from Asia and Australia through his proposed border. The line that was later given the name Wallace's Line extends from the Philippine Sea to the Indian Ocean. It represents the unanticipated animal distribution on both sides. On one side of the border, numerous mammal, bird, and aquatic species can be found in large numbers, while they are absent entirely on the other.

He wrote a number of academic papers, two books (1853: Palm Trees of the Amazon and Their Uses and Narrative of Travels on the Amazon and Rio Negro), a map showing the path of the Rio Negro, and other scientific articles. He received praise for these from the Royal Geographical Society. He also produced Contributions to the Theory of Natural Selection (1870) and The Malay Archipelago: The Land of the Orang-Utan, and the Bird of Paradise (1869), a highly successful account of his travels. Wallace split with scientific naturalism in the latter volume and in numerous papers from this time period on human evolution and spiritualism by asserting that natural selection could not account for the higher capabilities of humans.

THE REVOLUTION OF 1789

The slogan "Liberté, Egalité, Fraternité" originally arose during the French Revolution and is a holdover from the Age of Enlightenment. Even though it was frequently questioned, it finally became established during the Third Republic.

The Estates General in 1789 marked the beginning of the French Revolution, which lasted until the establishment of the French Consulate in November of 1799. During this time, France saw significant political and social change. While the institutions and values it established continue to be important in French political debate, many of its concepts are regarded as fundamental elements of liberal democracy.

The Ancien Régime's inability to control the disparities in society and the economy is frequently seen as one of the primary reasons for the French Revolution. Economic depression, unemployment, and high food prices were caused by rapid population increase and the inability to appropriately finance government debt. It led to a crisis that Louis XVI was unable to handle due to a regressive tax structure, elite hostility to reform, and other factors.

Between the late Middle Ages (about 1500) and the French Revolution that ended the monarchical rule of the French aristocracy (1790), the Ancien Régime, referred to as the Old Regime served as a societal and political framework for the Kingdom of France.

Regarding the causes of the French Revolution, historians have a lot of debate. They often admit the existence of a number of connected elements; however, they differ in the relative importance they accord to each one. These variables include societal transformation, financial and economic hardships, cultural shifts typically attributed to the Enlightenment and the political choices made by the parties concerned. Three families or classes dominated French society for many years.

- Clergy made up the first estate, the most affluent social class.
- The nobility made up the second estate.
- The ordinary people made up the third estate. It included businessmen, merchants, judges, attorneys, peasants, laborers who were not owners of the land, and servants.

Together, the first two classes made up 10% of the total population. 90% was the third estate. The third estate covered the cost of every kind of tax. The old French proverb "The Nobles fight, the clergy prays, and the commoners pay" served as the foundation of the society. The clergy, nobility, and "commons" made up the first, second, and third sections of the Estates-General, respectively. The first two estates were able to outnumber the Third Estate because they each had their own seat and were essentially exempt from paying taxes, although each represented less than five percent of the population.

When Charles-Alexandre de Calonne, the national controller of finances, organized the convening of an assembly of "notables" (prelates, great nobles, and certain members of the bourgeoisie) in February 1787 to discuss reforms intended to reduce the budget deficit by raising taxes for the privileged classes, the French Revolution began to take shape. The Estates-General, a body that had not met since 1614 and represented the ruling class, the clergy, and the commoners, was offered as a replacement by the assembly after it refused to accept responsibility for the reforms. The so-called "revolt of the aristocratic bodies" was the result of efforts made by Calonne's followers to impose fiscal changes in the face of opposition from the favored classes.

The poor crop in the years preceding 1789 was maybe a bigger challenge. Since there was significantly less bread due to these harvests, prices increased. The cost of bread had increased to historic highs by 1789, and the typical working-class individual was devoting as much as 80 percent of their salary to buying bread. On July 14, 1789, the day of the Bastille storming, bread prices reached their highest level ever recorded.

Despite the fact that the Third Estate constituted the large majority of the French population, one of the issues was whether all the estates should have an equal number of votes. To correct this, the Third Estate established a National Assembly under the tenet of a single vote for each representative, granting them an overwhelming percentage of votes and the opportunity to implement significant reforms. In the Tennis Court Oath, the National Assembly promised to draft an amended constitution for France and proclaimed itself the National Constituent Assembly.

Even if they were unfounded, the deputies' anxieties were reasonable, and the significance of the oath transcends its circumstances. The vow was an act of defiance that asserted that the population and the representatives they chose, not the king, were the true source of political power. Louis XVI was compelled by their unity to order the clergy and aristocracy to become part of the Third Estate in the National Assembly in order to create the appearance that he was in charge of the body. This oath was crucial to the Third Estate because it served as a protest that granted the Estates-General, each subsequent governing body, more authority.

The Tennis Court Oath

The National Assembly,

Considering that it has been called to establish the constitution of the realm, to bring about the regeneration of public order, and to maintain the true principles of monarchy, nothing may prevent it from continuing its deliberations in any place it is forced to establish itself; and, finally, the National Assembly exists wherever its members are gathered.

Decrees that all members of this Assembly immediately take a solemn oath never to separate and to reassemble wherever circumstances require until the constitution of the realm is established and fixed upon solid foundations; and that said oath having been sworn, all members and each one individually confirms this unwavering resolution with his signature.

We swear never to separate ourselves from the National Assembly and to reassemble wherever circumstances require until the constitution of the realm is drawn up and fixed upon solid foundations.

Parisians successfully besieged the Bastille, a historic castle that had served as a state jail since 1659, due to worries that King Louis XVI would detain France's newly formed National Assembly. The incident rapidly became a representation of the revolutionary fight since it represented a win by common Parisians over a conspicuous example of the king's coercive power.

First, soldiers were sent to surround Paris; many of them were mercenaries, and the majority believed that if the monarch gave the order to fire, they would do so without hesitation. On June 1, 30,000 soldiers were stationed outside the city. Second, the king dismissed a number of ministers and advisers, notably Jacques Necker, a well-liked liberal reformer who supported the Third Estate. These measures raised anxiety that the king might step in and bring apart the National Assembly or take over the streets of Paris violently.

People poured into the fortress, freed the seven inmates, took the gunpowder, and took the weapons away from the soldiers. In the confrontation, 98 invaders and one *invalide* (injured and disabled soldiers) are thought to have perished. Soon after the battle, the victorious side executed three more *invalides*, two Swiss Guardsmen, and de Launay's three officers by lynching. The governor was being executed by his savage prisoners when he purposely kicked one of them in the groin while they were still contemplating how to do it.

In Versailles, King Louis XVI decided two days later to reinstall his chief minister, Jacques Necker, who was fired for failing to try to obstruct the development of the National Assembly. This decision was influenced by the news of the Bastille's fall. However, despite the king's U-turn, the nation continued to descend into full-fledged upheaval.

The ascension of the common working class to the status of powerful revolutionaries was one of the major repercussions of the Bastille's storming during the French Revolution. Since they wore long pants rather than the knee-breeches or culottes that the wealthy preferred, they were known as sans-culottes, which is French for "without breeches."

Up until this time, the Third Estate's wealthiest bourgeoisie representatives had orchestrated the revolution's actions. The revolution had been propelled forward in large part by the lower classes.

The Bastille's fall signified the end of the old order, just as it was targeted in part because of its symbolic association with the king and the old order.

Even though Louis XVI nominally still held the throne of France, he was manifestly out of control. His reinstatement of Necker demonstrated that he was now vulnerable to popular expectations. Any chance of suppressing public aspirations or putting an end to the revolution was now gone. Many noblemen fled France totally after the Bastille was stormed, moving to Italy alongside other nearby nations.

The rise and fall of post-revolution Napolean Bonaparte

Napoleon supported the Revolution despite his duties as a French commander, seeing it as a realization of the Enlightenment ideas he had come to believe in and a victory of logic and reason. Nevertheless, he carried out his military duty and made 33 arrests while helping to put down a disturbance at Auxonne a week after the Bastille was overthrown.

The significant French naval base of Toulon, that fell under the authority of a British-led force in 1793, was one place where the royalists were gaining prominence. Napoleon had the chance to show off his military prowess and distinguish himself during the French-Republican attempts to regain that city. He had joined General Carteaux's army in July of the same year in an effort to stem the royalist flood that was engulfing the southern part of France.

As another royalist revolt broke out, Napoleon was summoned back to Paris for the defense of the government. He contributed to the suppression of the revolt in 1795 by strategic command and the placement of cannons on the streets of the city. After that, he established the legitimacy of the emerging French government, which consisted of five people, one of which was Barras.

Napoleon was appointed chief of the French military at the Italian front, referred to as the Army of Italy, as payment for his efforts in Paris. He moved swiftly, striking northeast and starting to push the Austrians and their coalition partners toward the Alps. This sparked a historic battle at Rivoli in January 1797, as the French ultimately triumphed over the Austrians.

Napoleon's journey to Egypt was foiled awry, and when he came to France in 1799, the French administration was in ruins. All three countries had declared war on it: Austria, Britain, and Russia. Napoleon assisted in organizing the 18 Brumaire coups in November 1799, profiting from this chaos and the allegiance of his army.

Now, Napoleon started to put some of his greatest feats away from the battlefield into motion. In an effort to mend the papacy's wounds from the repercussions of the revolution, he struck a Concordat with the Vatican. The Catholic pastors in France whose possessions were stolen during the Revolution were to receive wages from the French government, according to this concordat.

He established a number of committees, and over the course of several years, the Civil Code of the French People was written. The Napoleonic Code, which explained the regulations of the French Revolution, was created. It was implemented in France and areas of Germany and Italy that were under French authority, as well as in Belgium and Luxembourg. But a dictator's power was needed to carry out these measures. Napoleon organized a public vote that declared him emperor on May 18, 1804. Napoleon then invited the Pope to Paris to attend his crowning in December, when he first crowned himself before appointing his wife Josephine as her successor.

This crowning led to the formation of the Third Coalition, an anti-French coalition that included, among others, Britain, Austria, and Russia. Although the Russians and Austrians advanced with about 500,000 soldiers each, Napoleon had complete control of the French Empire's apparatus and could use it to deadly effect. With the infamous declaration, "I am the French Revolution," he amassed an army of almost 200,000 across the Rhine River and proceeded east, achieving a victory at Ulm. He continued on toward the area of Austerlitz, whence the Russian and Austrian armies withdrew in 1805. In the end, the Third Coalition disintegrated.

However, issues, particularly with the Russians, were never entirely resolved. Tsar Alexander I perceived a direct threat in this. Napoleon had 650 000 soldiers under his command and prepared to launch an assault by May 1812. The army that moved to Moscow proved exceptionally hard to supply when the French invasion finally materialized the following month because thousands of Napoleon's soldiers were already engaged in a conflict with Spain. Napoleon's army's combat capacity significantly decreased as a result of the Russians' successful defensive fighting and the severe winter in Russia. Russia and Prussia formed a coalition against Napoleon in February 1813; Austria would later join.

These Allies eventually drove Napoleon from Paris through a difficult battle that spanned over Germany and France, and they took control of the French capital in March 1814. He was banished to the Mediterranean island of Elba by the Treaty of Fontainebleau, which was signed in April.

When Napoleon made his way to France from Elba in 1815, he quickly regained power. The British and Prussian chiefs were Napoleon's only two adversaries present at the time, so he promptly put his plan into action.

In June 1815, the French, numbering 125,000, ambushed the commanders of the Allies. Blücher, the Prussian chief, stayed close enough to reinforce his friends while Wellington, the British duke, fled north to an advantageous position at Waterloo. On June 18, the Allied forces were on the verge of defeat when Napoleon was taken by surprise. Napoleon made the decision to resign after this defeat, which was his final one. He was transported to St. Helena, a rugged island in the South Atlantic, where he lived in exile and died in 1821.

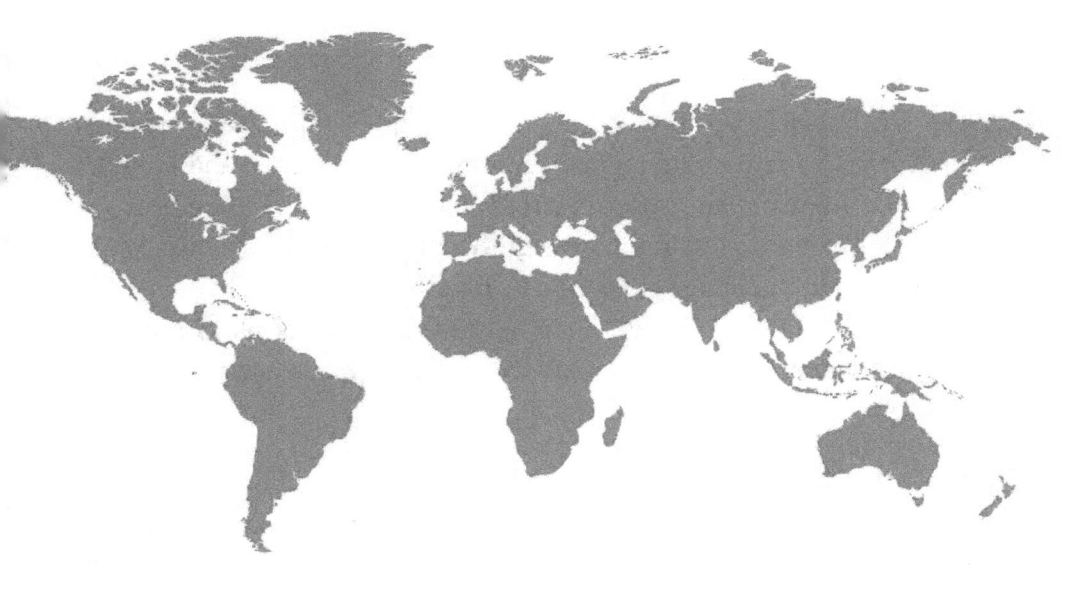

The Distance Between Us: Pangaea

Around 240 million years ago, Pangaea was a real place. Approximately 200 million years back, this one giant continent started to fragment. Pangaea split into fragments over the course of millions of years, and each piece migrated away from the other.

The Earth's surface is divided into seven major landmasses, known as continents, each with its unique geography, ecosystems, and cultures. These continents are spread across the planet, and their varying distances from one another have significant impacts on various aspects of our world, including geopolitics, climate patterns, biodiversity, and human interactions. The distance between continents plays a pivotal role in shaping the planet's dynamics, and its impacts are far-reaching and complex.

The distance between continents has profound geopolitical implications. Historically, the vast oceans and expanses of land separating continents have acted as natural barriers, influencing the development of civilizations and shaping the course of human history. The distances between continents have often determined trade routes, migration patterns, and political alliances.

For instance, the separation between Europe and the Americas played a pivotal role in the Age of Exploration. The vast Atlantic Ocean necessitated long and perilous sea voyages, leading to the discovery of new lands, the colonization of the Americas, and the exchange of goods, ideas, and diseases between the Old World and the New World.

Similarly, the separation of Asia and Europe by the expanse of land known as the Eurasian landmass has influenced the interactions between different cultures and civilizations. The Silk Road, an ancient network of trade routes, connected these distant regions and facilitated the exchange of goods, technologies, and cultural practices.

The distance between continents significantly affects climate patterns and biodiversity. The Earth's climate is influenced by the distribution of land and water, which in turn is influenced by the arrangement and distances between continents. Ocean currents, prevailing winds, and temperature gradients are all impacted by the geographical layout of continents.

The varying distances between continents contribute to the creation of different climate zones and ecosystems. For example, the isolation of

Australia, which is surrounded by vast stretches of ocean, has led to the evolution of unique and diverse flora and fauna that are found nowhere else on Earth. Similarly, the separation of Africa from South America by the Atlantic Ocean allowed for the development of distinct ecosystems and species on each continent.

Advancements in transportation and communication technology have reduced the perceived distance between continents, enabling rapid and frequent interactions between people from different parts of the world. Air travel, internet connectivity, and international trade have made it easier for individuals, goods, and information to traverse great distances.

The shrinking of the world due to improved connectivity has led to increased cultural exchange, international collaborations, and a globalized economy. People can now communicate, share ideas, and conduct business with counterparts on different continents as if they were in the same city. This interconnectedness has both positive and negative impacts, fostering understanding and cooperation but also posing challenges related to cultural identity and economic inequality.

The distance between continents also has ecological implications, particularly in the context of invasive species and ecosystem disruptions. Human activities, such as trade and travel, have facilitated the unintentional introduction of non-native species to new continents. These invasive species can outcompete native species, disrupt local ecosystems, and lead to ecological imbalances.

For example, the brown tree snake, native to Australia, was accidentally introduced to the Pacific island of Guam, where it has caused significant ecological damage by preying on native bird species and leading to population declines. Similarly, the spread of invasive species like zebra mussels in North America and rabbits in Australia highlights the far-reaching consequences of human-induced ecological disruptions across continents.

The distance between continents is not merely a geographical concept; it is a dynamic force that shapes the course of history, influences climate and biodiversity, facilitates human interactions, and affects ecological systems. As our world becomes increasingly interconnected and globalized, understanding the impacts of these distances becomes essential for addressing challenges related to geopolitics, environmental conservation, and cultural exchange. The intricate web of relationships between continents serves as a reminder of the interconnectedness of all life on Earth and the importance of responsible stewardship of our planet.

Continental Drift

One of the first hypotheses put up by geologists for how continents might migrate through time is called continental drift. The modern understanding of plate tectonics has now supplanted the theory of drifting continents.

The scientist Alfred Wegener is most closely connected with the concept of continental drift. Wegener wrote a paper outlining his notion that the continents were "drifting" across the Earth, occasionally crashing across oceans and into one another, in the beginning of the twentieth century. He referred to it as continental drift.

Today's scientists believe that a number of supercontinents, including Pangaea, have formed and fragmented during the Earth's history. These include Rodinia, which predated Pannotia by over one billion years, and Pannotia, which emerged roughly 600 million years ago.

The continental drift idea proposed by Wegener was rejected by scientists. The mechanism underlying the theory's operation—specifically, the reasons why the continents drifted and the patterns they followed—was one of its key components. Wegener hypothesized that the continents may have moved toward and away from one another as a result of the Earth's rotation. (This is false.)

The continents on opposing sides of the ridge drift apart as the seafloor widens. The Mid-Atlantic Ridge, for instance, divides the North

American and Eurasian tectonic plates. At a distance of roughly 2 centimeters (1 inch) every year, these two continents are drifting apart.

The locations of rift valleys are where a continent is rupturing. Africa will eventually divide over the Great Rift Valley system, for instance. The continent that is currently one will split into two, with one portion landing on the African plate and the other on the less massive Somali plate. The Horn of Africa and Madagascar will be the new Somali continent's two largest landmasses, and the majority of it will be oceanic. The primary geologic forces that contributed to what Wegener called continental drift were these activities.

What will happen if the continents collide?

When continents collide, a geological phenomenon known as continental collision or continent-continent collision occurs. This collision can lead to a range of complex and impactful geological, tectonic, and topographical changes. The collision of continents is a slow process that takes millions of years, and its effects can shape the Earth's surface and create dramatic landscapes.

One of the most significant results of continent collisions is the formation of mountain ranges. When two continental plates collide, the immense pressure and force exerted to cause the Earth's crust to buckle and fold, leading to the uplift of the crust and the creation of towering mountain ranges. The collision between the Indian Plate and the Eurasian Plate, for example, gave rise to the Himalayas, the highest mountain range in the world.

Continental collisions are associated with increased seismic activity. As the plates collide and the crust is compressed, stress builds up along faults and fractures in the Earth's crust. This stress can be released suddenly in the form of earthquakes. Some of the world's most powerful earthquakes have occurred in regions undergoing a continental collision, as the accumulated strain is suddenly released.

When two continents collide, the immense pressure and heat generated by the collision can cause the melting of the Earth's crust, leading to the formation of magma. This magma can find its way to the surface, resulting in volcanic eruptions.

Continental collisions can have significant impacts on global climate patterns and ocean currents. The uplift of mountain ranges can influence the distribution of rainfall and create rain shadows, where one side of a mountain range is lush and wet while the other side is dry. Additionally, the changes in the arrangement of landmasses resulting from collisions can affect ocean currents and consequently influence climate patterns on a larger scale.

THE FOUNDING FATHERS OF THE USA

The Declaration of Independence, the republican form of government outlined in the United States Constitution, and the Founding Fathers, the most illustrious statesmen of America's Revolutionary generation, were all products of the Founding Generation. They were also responsible for the successful war to win American colonies' independence from Great Britain.

The Founders are portrayed as either noble heroes or malevolent demons, as the architects of everything good or evil in American civilization. The debate surrounding the Founders of the United States holds a unique place in American history, unlike anything seen in the history of European nation-states. Firstly, the United States wasn't founded on shared ethnicity, language, or religion that could be assumed as the core source of national identity. Instead, it was established on a set of beliefs and principles, often referred to as "self-evident truths" by Thomas Jefferson, which were declared in 1776 and later enshrined in the Bill of Rights of the Constitution. Becoming an American citizen isn't determined by one's ancestry or genealogy but rather by embracing and endorsing these founding values, which grants those who articulated these values a special significance.

Secondly, the American legal system connects all major constitutional decisions to the language of the Constitution itself and frequently to the "original intent" of the framers. This legal tradition underscores the enduring relevance of the American Founders in contemporary discussions of both domestic and foreign policy—a significance that would be hard to imagine in many European nations.

In its most fundamental sense, the Founders of the United States established the first modern nation-state grounded in liberal principles. They championed the idea that political authority in any government should reside within the citizenry, as opposed to being vested in a monarchy sanctioned by divine authority. The Founders advocated for the notion that economic prosperity is reliant on the free play of individual talents and efforts within the marketplace rather than being dictated by state-controlled policies. They emphasized the importance of the individual, positioning the individual as the paramount entity in the political equation rather than subordinating them to society or the state. They upheld the principle that all citizens should be treated equally before the law, regardless of their background or social status.

Furthermore, this liberal framework has emerged as the preferred political model for success in the modern world. It proved to be instrumental in defeating European monarchies in the 19th century and countering the totalitarian regimes of Germany, Japan, and the Soviet Union in the 20th century.

In a more detailed analysis, the Founding Fathers accomplished four remarkable feats that defied conventional wisdom. They successfully secured independence from the most formidable military and economic superpower of their time, marking an unprecedented victory in a war for colonial autonomy. They pioneered the creation of the first large-scale republic in the modern world, a groundbreaking experiment in governance. They introduced the concept of political parties, which institutionalized the notion of a legitimate opposition within a democratic system. They laid the groundwork for the separation of church and state as a fundamental principle, even though it took several decades for this principle to be fully implemented in all states.

It's worth noting that these accomplishments were achieved without resorting to violent purges like the guillotine or firing squad, which were tragically seen in subsequent revolutions in France, Russia, and China.

The Fathers

The Founding Fathers of the United States were a group of prominent leaders, thinkers, and statesmen who played a pivotal role in the American Revolution and the establishment of the United States as an independent nation. While there were many individuals who contributed to the founding of the United States, some of the most well-known Founding Fathers include:

1. George Washington: Washington was not only the Commander-in-Chief of the Continental Army during the American Revolution but also a unifying figure in the early days of the United States. He presided over the Constitutional Convention in 1787 and became the country's first President in 1789. His leadership helped establish the precedent of a peaceful transfer of power in a democratic republic.

2. Thomas Jefferson: As the primary author of the Declaration of Independence, Jefferson articulated the colonies' reasons for seeking independence from British rule. He later served as the third President and is known for the Louisiana Purchase, which doubled the size of the United States.

3. Benjamin Franklin: Franklin was a polymath who made significant contributions to science, inventing the lightning rod and bifocal glasses. He also played a crucial role in diplomacy, negotiating the Treaty of Alliance with France in 1778, which secured French support for the American cause.

4. John Adams: Adams was a fervent advocate for independence and helped draft the Massachusetts Constitution in 1780, which became a model for the U.S. Constitution. He was a key diplomat in Europe during the Revolution and served as the second President, overseeing the passage of the Alien and Sedition Acts.

5. Alexander Hamilton: Hamilton's influence was profound, particularly in economic matters. He authored many of the Federalist Papers, advocating for the ratification of the U.S. Constitution. As the first Secretary of the Treasury, he established the nation's financial system and founded the first national bank.

6. James Madison: Madison's contributions to the Constitutional Convention were pivotal. He took meticulous notes during the Convention's deliberations, which provided a valuable record of the proceedings. Madison also co-authored the Federalist Papers and played a critical role in drafting the Bill of Rights.

7. John Jay: Jay was not only a co-author of the Federalist Papers but also a skilled diplomat. He negotiated the Treaty of Paris in 1783, which ended the American Revolutionary War, and he served as the first Chief Justice of the United States.

8. George Mason: Mason was a strong advocate for individual rights and played a significant role in shaping Virginia's Constitution. His ideas influenced the Bill of Rights, and his work on the Virginia Declaration of Rights emphasized principles such as freedom of the press and the prohibition of cruel and unusual punishment.

9. Thomas Paine: Paine's pamphlets, such as "Common Sense," were instrumental in rallying public sentiment for independence. His writings provided clear, persuasive arguments for breaking away from British rule and helped galvanize the colonial population.

These are just a few of the Founding Fathers who made significant contributions to the establishment of the United States as an independent nation. Their ideas, writings, and leadership played a vital role in shaping the nation's government, institutions, and principles.

Numerous additional people performed minor but equally important roles during the formation, in addition to the known seven, who made significant contributions. Just a few of them include George Mason, Patrick Henry, John Hancock, John Marshall, and Samuel Adams. The United States Constitution had 39 signers, but the Declaration of Independence had 56. Women, like Mercy Otis Warren and Abigail Adams, also had significant roles in addition to the men who performed them.

The common perception of the Founding Fathers as a unified group that seamlessly worked together to establish a single American nation oversimplifies the reality. In truth, they held vastly divergent viewpoints on a wide array of issues, including the extent of federal government powers, the contentious matter of slavery, and the degree of radicalism or moderation in the American Revolution. These disparities in opinion often strained relationships and, in some instances, posed a significant threat to the cohesion of the emerging nation.

This small collection of men, more than any other group in history, distilled decades of enlightenment philosophy into a type of government that aimed to curtail centralized power, safeguard citizens' rights, and guarantee the consent of the governed. They dedicated their lives, their wealth, and their holy honor in order to do this. We still hold fast to the values they put into practice.

Madiba: Black Pimpernel

Nelson Mandela, referred to as the "Black Pimpernel" due to his clever evasion of authorities in various disguises, has emerged as a powerful icon of the African struggle for freedom. Hailing from a prominent family, he initially pursued a career in law but progressively deepened his engagement in politics. His journey began with the African

National Congress under the leadership of Nobel Peace Prize laureate Chief Albert Luthuli.

Nelson Mandela's revolution was not just about changing the political landscape of South Africa; it was about changing hearts and minds. His legacy of forgiveness, reconciliation, and perseverance continues to inspire people worldwide, reminding us that even in the face of seemingly insurmountable odds, positive change is possible through dialogue, understanding, and a steadfast commitment to justice. Nelson Mandela's revolution remains a shining example of what one person can achieve when driven by the ideals of freedom, equality, and human dignity.

Of course, the name Mandela now carries a special significance for people all around the world. They relate Mandela to liberty, equality, and justice. Mandela has come to represent civil rights, peace, and wisdom, among other things. Millions of people who would be happy to see Mandela beatified have elevated him to the status of a saint despite the fact that, according to his own acceptance, he is far from being eligible for any kind of canonization. Mandela has nearly become a religious figure. He frequently expressed the opinion that he had lived a "thoroughly immoral life," but he was never willing to go into specifics. What, then, was he discussing?

Nelson Mandela was the Xhosa-speaking Tembu people's son, descended from Chief Henry Mandela of the Madiba tribe. Young Nelson was brought up by Jongintaba, the Tembu regent, after the passing of his father. To pursue a career as a lawyer, Nelson gave up his right to the chieftainship. He went to South African Native College, which became the University of Fort Hare, and the University of the Witwatersrand, where he studied law. He later passed the bar test to become a lawyer. He entered the African National Congress (ANC), a movement for Black liberation, in 1944 and rose to the position of youth league leader. He met and wed Evelyn Ntoko Mase in the same year. Mandela later held further senior posts within the ANC, where he worked to reenergize the group and fight against apartheid.

Mandela founded South Africa's first Black law firm in Johannesburg in 1952 with fellow ANC member Oliver Tambo, focusing on matters arising from the post-1948 racist laws. Mandela also played a significant role at the beginning of a movement of rebellion against South Africa's pass laws, which mandated that non-whites carry documents (referred to as passbooks or reference books) enabling their entry in areas the government deemed "restricted" (i.e., typically reserved for the white population). For this movement, he traveled around the nation to garner support for peaceful ways to protest discriminatory legislation. He contributed to the Freedom Charter's writing in 1955, which called for nonracial democratic rule in the Republic of South Africa.

Mandela was frequently targeted by the authorities as a result of his anti-apartheid activism. He was intermittently prohibited (severe restrictions on movement, association, and speech) beginning in 1952.

Mandela renounced his nonviolent attitude and started encouraging acts of disruption against the South African government in the wake of the 1960 Sharpeville killing of innocent Black South Africans by police, which led to the ANC's eventual banning. One of the founding members of Umkhonto we Sizwe ("Spear of the Nation"), the ANC's military wing, he fled into hiding and earned the nickname "Black Pimpernel" for his skill in avoiding capture. He traveled to Algeria in 1962 to receive instruction in sabotage and guerilla warfare before getting back to South Africa the following year. Mandela was detained at a roadblock in Natal on August 5, not long after his homecoming, and was later given a five-year prison term.

He was detained in December 1956, together with over 100 other persons, on treason allegations intended to intimidate anti-apartheid campaigners. In the same year, Mandela was put on trial and ultimately found not guilty in 1961. He wed Nomzamo Winifred Madikizela after divorcing his first wife during the protracted legal proceedings. The infamous Rivonia Trial, named after a posh suburb of Johannesburg where police found a large amount of ammunition and other supplies at the headquarters of the hidden Umkhonto we Sizwe, took place in October 1963. The trial involved incarcerated Mandela and numerous men and was held for sabotage, treachery, and destructive conspiracy.

Mandela was detained in the offshore Robben Island Prison from 1964 to 1982. He was then held at the high-security Pollsmoor Prison till 1988, while following tuberculosis treatment, he was moved to the Victor Verster Prison close to Paarl.

Mandela maintained strong support from the Black population of South Africa throughout his imprisonment, and the foreign society that opposed apartheid made his captivity a cause célèbre. Ministers in the administration of President P.W. Botha engaged him in exploratory talks as South Africa's political scenario worsened following 1983 and especially after 1988. In December 1989, he met with Botha's successor, de Klerk.

Mandela was freed from jail by the South African government, led by President de Klerk, on February 11, 1990. Mandela was selected to serve as the ANC's deputy president soon after his release. In July 1991, he was elected party president. To put an end to apartheid and ensure an orderly shift to nonracial governance in South Africa, Mandela headed the ANC in talks with de Klerk.

Mandela presided over South Africa for five years. One of his accomplishments was the establishment of South Africa's Truth and Reconciliation Commission, whose goal was to record human rights abuses and assist both victims and perpetrators in accepting their history. Although its findings are disputed, the committee gave a country still suffering from centuries' worth of wounds the first steps toward restorative justice—a procedure that emphasizes restoration rather than revenge.

Mandela and President de Klerk received the Nobel Peace Prize in 1993 for their efforts to end apartheid. South Africans of color and whites successfully negotiated. South Africa conducted its inaugural democratic elections on April 27, 1994. With 62.65% of the vote, the ANC dominated the election. Mandela sought to prevent the collapse of South Africa's economy while he was president. Apartheid's economic legacy, which included poverty, inequality, unequal availability of public amenities and infrastructure, including a financial system that had been in trouble for almost two decades, also required urgent attention.

Mandela also utilized the nation's love of sports as a major selling point to get white South Africans to back the once-despised predominantly white national rugby team as part of his goal for peace, nation-building, and reconciliation. The Rugby World Cup that South Africa hosted in 1995 propelled the new Republic of South Africa onto the international scale and increased its reputation. South Africa won the Rugby World Cup, which was the first one in which every game was played in a single nation. A fresh charter for the country was enacted by Mandela in 1996; it established a powerful centralized government built around a majority vote and protected both minorities' rights and the right to freedom of speech.

Mandela actively promoted fund-raising campaigns for the Nelson Mandela Children's Fund in South Africa. He would accomplish this, among other things, by encouraging business executives to accompany him on visits to poor people's settlements, where he would solicit their pledges of money, especially for classrooms and schools. These buildings are now referred to as "Madiba magic" creations.

Jack, The Individualist mind: John F Kennedy

Jack, also known by the nickname John, held the position of the second eldest among a remarkable group of nine siblings. Among his brothers and sisters were Eunice Kennedy Shriver, the founder of the Special Olympics; Robert Kennedy, who served as the U.S. Attorney General. And Ted

Kennedy, a highly influential figure in American history as one of the most powerful senators.

Early in life, JFK experienced wealth and a heavy focus on education. Before enrolling at Harvard University, he attended the Connecticut-based Choate School, where he excelled academically and as an active participant in several organizations and societies. "Why England Slept," Kennedy's senior thesis, was eventually turned into a book.

During World War II, JFK enlisted in the US Navy following his graduation from Harvard in 1940. Serving with honor, he oversaw a patrol torpedo boat in the Pacific and was awarded the Navy and Marine Corps Medal for his valor and leadership after his ship was sunk.

Kennedy's upbringing set the stage for his eventual political career, which was distinguished by a combination of wealth, curiosity, and dedication to public service. His family history and his service in the Navy both shaped his personality and leadership abilities.

William Randolph Hearst was a friend of Kennedy's father, who set up his son's job as an exclusive reporter for Hearst Newspapers in April 1945. The job kept his name in the spotlight and "exposed him to media as a potential profession." That May, he flew to Berlin a second time as a correspondent to cover the Potsdam Conference and other events.

In 1946, John F. Kennedy (JFK) made his official political debut by contesting for the US House of Representatives. He was chosen to represent Massachusetts's eleventh congressional district in Congress, a position he held from January 3, 1947, until January 3, 1953. He belonged to the Democratic Party at this time.

As Kennedy was elected to the U.S. Senate in 1952, his political career took off. From January 3, 1953, until his election as the 35th President of the United States of America in 1961, he served as the senator from Massachusetts. Once more, he was a Democrat all the way through his Senate career.

In 1946, JFK was elected as a Democrat to the U.S. House of Representatives from Massachusetts's 11th congressional district. He served three terms in the House, distinguishing himself through his articulate speeches and contributions to foreign policy discussions.

John F. Kennedy's decision to run for the presidency in 1960 was influenced by a combination of personal ambition, a desire to contribute to public service, and the encouragement of his political advisors. JFK came from a family with a strong tradition of public service and political involvement. His father, Joseph P. Kennedy, was a successful businessman and former ambassador, and his older brother, Joe Jr., had been groomed for a political career before his tragic death during World War II. John felt a sense of duty and saw political leadership as a way to continue the family legacy.

Kennedy's early success in the House of Representatives and later in the Senate raised his national profile. He became a rising star within the Democratic Party, gaining attention for his charisma, oratory skills, and positions on various issues. His role in foreign affairs, including his criticism of the Eisenhower administration's handling of the Cold War, contributed to his image as a leader with a strong understanding of international relations. His experiences and views on global issues enhanced his appeal as a potential president during a time of heightened Cold War tensions.

The Democratic Party saw Kennedy as a charismatic and potentially electable candidate. He faced strong competition within the party during the primaries, notably from Hubert Humphrey and Lyndon B. Johnson, but he was able to secure the nomination. Kennedy recognized the changing dynamics of American society in the 1960s. His youth and fresh perspective contrasted with the older, more established political figures of the time. He presented himself as a new and dynamic leader, offering a vision for progress and change.

The advent of televised debates played a crucial role in Kennedy's decision to run for president. His confident and composed demeanor in the debates helped him connect with voters on a personal level and contributed significantly to his electoral success. The 1960 presidential campaign was historic for its televised debates, where Kennedy's charisma and telegenic appeal contrasted with Nixon's more reserved demeanor. Kennedy's New Frontier platform included proposals for civil rights, healthcare, and economic policies to stimulate growth.

Kennedy's inaugural address emphasized the importance of civic engagement and service to the nation. He brought a new generation's perspective to the presidency, emphasizing a sense of optimism and a commitment to progress.

The huge Fitzgerald family Bible was held by a US Supreme Court clerk on January 20, 1961, the day John F. Kennedy swore the pledge of office to become the 35th president of the United States. Over twenty thousand attendees gathered in the 20-degree weather on the east-facing front of the Capitol to see the ceremony against a backdrop of heavy snow and sunshine. Kennedy gave what has come to be seen as a historic inaugural speech after taking off his topcoat and displaying both youth and vigor.

Kennedy's plea for all Americans to dedicate themselves to sacrifice and duty toward the close of the speech—"And so, my fellow Americans: ask not what your country can do for you - ask what you can do for your country"—is often regarded as the speech's most memorable and enduring passage. "My fellow citizens of the world: ask not what America will do for you, but what together we can do for the freedom of man," he said, continuing to address his global audience.

Here is a quick glimpse at his presidential tenure:

1. **Bay of Pigs Invasion**: Early in his presidency, Kennedy faced the Bay of Pigs Invasion, a failed attempt by Cuban exiles to overthrow Fidel Castro. The incident had lasting consequences but also showcased Kennedy's ability to take responsibility for the failure.

2. **Cuban Missile Crisis (1962):** One of the most critical moments of the Cold War occurred when the U.S. and the Soviet Union faced off over the placement of nuclear missiles in Cuba.

Kennedy's measured response and negotiation skills are widely credited with diffusing the crisis.

3. **Space Race and Moon Landing (1961-1969):** Kennedy set the ambitious goal of landing an American on the moon before the end of the 1960s. This vision materialized with the Apollo 11 mission in 1969, fulfilling Kennedy's commitment to space exploration.

4. **Peace Corps (1961):** Kennedy established the Peace Corps, a volunteer program promoting cultural exchange and development assistance. The program has since become a symbol of American humanitarian efforts.

5. **Alliance for Progress (1961):** Kennedy launched the Alliance for Progress, a program aimed at promoting economic development and social justice in Latin American countries, fostering cooperation and stability in the region.

6. **Civil Rights Initiatives:** While progress on civil rights was slow during Kennedy's presidency, he expressed support for the cause. His administration took initial steps toward comprehensive civil rights legislation, which was later enacted under President Lyndon B. Johnson.

On November 22, 1963, President Kennedy, along with First Lady Jacqueline Kennedy, Texas Governor John Connally, and his wife Nellie, started their motorcade from Love Field Airport and proceeded through the streets of Dallas. As the motorcade entered Dealey Plaza, shots rang out. The shots were fired from a sixth-floor window of the Texas School Book Depository building.

At approximately 12:30 p.m. Central Standard Time, Kennedy was struck by two bullets. The first bullet hit him in the upper back, and the second, fatal shot struck him in the head. Governor John Connally, sitting in the same car as Kennedy, was also hit by gunfire. He survived but sustained serious injuries.

Kennedy received emergency medical treatment at Parkland Hospital, where he was pronounced dead 30 minutes later, at 1:00 p.m. (CST). At the time of his assassination, he was 46 years old and had served as president for 1,036 days. Lee Harvey Oswald, an order filler at the Texas School Book Depository, the site from which the shots were fired, was arrested for the murder of police officer J.D. Tippit and subsequently charged with Kennedy's assassination. Oswald denied any involvement, asserting that he was a scapegoat, and was shot dead by Jack Ruby on November 24 before facing prosecution. Ruby, in turn, was arrested and convicted for Oswald's murder. Although Ruby successfully appealed his conviction and death sentence, he succumbed to cancer on January 3, 1967, as plans for his new trial were being arranged.

Within hours of the assassination, Lee Harvey Oswald was arrested at the Texas Theatre in Dallas. He was initially taken into custody for the murder of a Dallas police officer, J.D. Tippit, and later became the prime suspect in Kennedy's assassination. The subsequent investigation, led by the Warren Commission, concluded that Oswald acted alone in assassinating President Kennedy.

President Johnson promptly issued an executive order establishing the Warren Commission, headed by Chief Justice Earl Warren, to probe the assassination. The commission's findings asserted that Oswald acted independently in the assassination of Kennedy and was not involved in any conspiracy. However, these findings are a subject of dispute among many. The assassination emerged as a critical juncture in U.S. history, influencing the nation profoundly and leading to consequential political consequences.

After Kennedy's assassination, his body was brought to Washington. On November 23, military pallbearers carried the flag-draped coffin into the White House's East Room, where it rested for 24 hours. Subsequently, the coffin, placed on a horse-drawn caisson, was taken to the Capitol for public viewing. Hundreds of thousands lined up to pay their respects during the 18-hour lying-in-state period, with a quarter million passing through the rotunda.

The funeral service occurred on November 25 at St. Matthew's Cathedral in Washington, D.C., led by Cardinal Richard Cushing. Approximately 1,200 guests, including representatives from over 90 countries, attended the Requiem Mass. Following the service, Kennedy was laid to rest at Arlington National Cemetery in Virginia.

Philosophia: Love of Wisdom

The term "philosophy" comes from this Greek word and has been used to describe the systematic and rational inquiry into the nature of existence, knowledge, ethics, and various other aspects of human experience. Ancient Greek philosophy profoundly influenced Western thought and laid the foundation for many branches of philosophy that are still studied and discussed today. Prominent Greek philosophers include Socrates, Plato, and Aristotle, among others.

Ancient Greece, particularly during the Classical period (5th to 4th centuries BCE), was a remarkable era in human history characterized by significant intellectual and philosophical advancements. This period was marked by city-states flourishing, including Athens, which became a hub for intellectual exchange and the birthplace of many influential philosophical ideas.

Greece was situated at the crossroads of Europe, Asia, and Africa, facilitating cultural and intellectual exchanges. The Greeks interacted with neighboring civilizations, including the Egyptians, Persians, and Mesopotamians, absorbing and synthesizing diverse cultural influences. This cross-pollination of ideas contributed to the richness of Greek thought.

The Greeks were exposed to the wisdom of earlier civilizations, such as the Egyptians and Babylonians. This exposure fueled an intellectual curiosity and a desire to understand the natural world, leading to early scientific and philosophical inquiry development. Thinkers like Socrates, Plato, and Aristotle investigated the nature of reality, ethics, politics, and the human condition. Their ideas, along with those of other philosophers, laid the groundwork for Western philosophy and had a lasting impact on the development of human thought.

Socrates:

Socrates was born in Athens around 469 BCE and is a foundational figure in Western philosophy. Although he left no written records of his own teachings, his impact is profound, thanks to the writings of his devoted student, Plato, and others he influenced.

Socrates' teaching method, known as the Socratic method or elenchus, was a distinctive form of cooperative argumentative dialogue. Instead of giving his students direct answers, Socrates engaged them in a series of questions designed to stimulate critical thinking and self-discovery. The goal was not to impart information but to help individuals recognize contradictions and inconsistencies in their own beliefs.

He often used irony to expose the limitations of human knowledge. Despite his reputation as one of the wisest men in Athens (as proclaimed by the Oracle at Delphi), Socrates maintained that he possessed no true wisdom. This humility was a central theme in his philosophy, emphasizing the importance of acknowledging one's ignorance as a starting point for intellectual growth.

He frequently referred to his "daimonion" or inner divine sign—a sort of internal guide or conscience. This aspect of his philosophy added a spiritual dimension, suggesting a connection to something beyond human understanding. The daimonion did not provide answers but served as a cautionary signal, steering Socrates away from actions that would lead to harm.

Although Socrates did not write down his teachings, his student, Plato, preserved his ideas and conversations. The dialogues Plato wrote, particularly those featuring Socrates as the main character, provide insight into Socratic philosophy.

His commitment to questioning societal norms and challenging traditional beliefs eventually led to his trial in 399 BCE. He was accused of impiety and corrupting the youth of Athens. Despite his defense during the trial, he was sentenced to death. Socrates chose to accept the verdict and drank hemlock, maintaining his philosophical principles until the end.

Plato:

Plato was born around 428 BCE into an aristocratic Athenian family and is one of the most influential philosophers in the Western tradition. A student of Socrates and a teacher of Aristotle, Plato's contributions to philosophy extend across a wide range of topics.

As a young man, Plato intended to pursue a career in politics, but his encounter with Socrates redirected his aspirations toward philosophy. Socrates' method of questioning and pursuit of deeper truths deeply impacted him, shaping his intellectual journey. Around 387 BCE, he founded the Academy in Athens, which is often considered the first institution of higher learning in the Western world. The Academy became a center for philosophical and scientific inquiry, attracting students from various regions. It played a crucial role in the transmission and development of philosophical ideas.

His philosophical ideas are primarily conveyed through dialogues, written in the form of conversations between Socrates and other characters. These dialogues have various philosophical themes, including ethics, metaphysics, epistemology, politics, and the nature of reality. Notable dialogues include "The Republic," "Symposium," and "Phaedo."

At the core of his metaphysical philosophy is the Theory of Forms (or Ideas). He posited that the physical world is an imperfect reflection of a higher realm of Forms, which are abstract, perfect, and eternal. For example, the Form of Justice exists independently of individual instances of justice in the world.

His impact extends to his student Aristotle, who went on to become one of history's greatest philosophers. While Aristotle disagreed with some of his ideas, particularly the Theory of Forms, he built upon Plato's foundation, contributing to the development of Western philosophy.

Aristotle:

Aristotle was born in 384 BCE in Stagira, a Greek colony in Macedonia, and is one of the most influential philosophers and polymaths in history. His wide-ranging contributions span philosophy, science, ethics, politics, and more. He became a student at Plato's Academy in Athens when he was around 17 years old. While Plato influenced him, Aristotle also developed his own philosophical ideas, often engaging in critical dialogue with his mentor.

After studying under Plato, Aristotle became the tutor to Alexander the Great, the future conqueror of much of the known world. This connection provided him with resources and opportunities to study a wide range of subjects, as Alexander's conquests exposed him to diverse cultures and natural environments.

His "Metaphysics" is a foundational work in philosophy, addressing the nature of existence, causality, and the ultimate reality. In contrast to Plato's Theory of Forms, he proposed a more empirical and systematic approach, emphasizing the study of the material world to understand the underlying principles of being.

His ethical philosophy is articulated in works like "Nicomachean Ethics." He introduced the concept of virtue ethics, highlighting the development of moral character through virtuous habits. He believed that ethical conduct is found between extremes, avoiding both deficiency and excess.

His contributions to the natural sciences are vast. In Physics, he presented theories on motion, causation, and the structure of the cosmos. His work in biology, as found in "On the Parts of Animals" and "The History of Animals," involved extensive classification and observation of living organisms.

His systematic and empirical approach laid the groundwork for scientific inquiry and the development of Western philosophy. His works were preserved and studied throughout the medieval period, influencing Islamic, Jewish, and Christian scholars. The rediscovery of Aristotle's writings during the Renaissance further fueled his impact on the evolution of modern thought.

Pythagoras:

Pythagoras was born in 570 BCE on the Samos islands in the Aegean Sea. A philosopher from ancient Greece renowned for his contributions to mathematics and for founding a religious movement that intertwined mathematical and philosophical ideas. He later established a school in the city of Croton in southern Italy, where he and his followers, known as the Pythagoreans, engaged in both intellectual and religious pursuits.

Pythagoras is best known for the Pythagorean Theorem, a fundamental principle in geometry that establishes the relationship between the sides of a right-angled triangle. This theorem has widespread applications in mathematics and physics.

His teachings extended beyond mathematics. He believed in the inherent harmony of the cosmos, expressing the idea that the mathematical relationships governing the physical world reflected a broader cosmic order. This perspective influenced later philosophers and scientists who sought to understand the universe through mathematical principles.

He is often credited with discovering the mathematical relationships underlying musical intervals. According to legend, he observed the harmony of sounds produced by hammers of varying weights, leading to the concept of numerical ratios governing musical harmony. This connection between music and mathematics contributed to the Pythagorean view of a harmonious universe.

He also introduced the concept of metempsychosis or the transmigration of souls. He believed in the cycle of reincarnation, where souls could be reborn into different bodies. This idea is linked to his views on the immortality of the soul, suggesting that the soul is eternal and undergoes a series of earthly lives. His influence extended to Plato and other philosophers who incorporated Pythagorean concepts into their own philosophical systems.

Heraclitus:

Heraclitus was a pre-Socratic philosopher born around 535 BCE in Ephesus, present-day Turkey, who greatly contributed to the philosophical landscape of ancient Greece. He is often characterized as the "philosopher of change" due to his emphasis on the dynamic and ever-changing nature of the universe.

His central tenet was encapsulated in the famous phrase "panta rhei," which translates to "everything flows" or "everything is in flux." He believed that change is not only a constant but the fundamental essence of the universe. He famously stated, "You cannot step into the same river twice," highlighting the perpetual flux and transformation of all things.

He posited the idea that opposites are not only interconnected but also necessary for the existence of each other. He expressed this concept with the well-known statement, "The path up and down are one and the same." This notion challenged the static and dualistic views of reality some of his contemporaries held.

He was critical of relying solely on the senses to understand reality. He believed that the senses provided an illusionary perception of stability, while true understanding required a deeper recognition of the underlying unity and constant change.

He introduced the concept of "logos," a term with rich and varied meanings in ancient Greek philosophy. In his context, logos represented an ordering principle, a rational structure underlying the universe. He argued that this logo governs the world, maintaining order amid the constant flux.

His cryptic and paradoxical statements have led to various interpretations, and some aspects of his philosophy remain open to debate. Scholars have grappled with the complexity of his ideas and the challenge of reconciling apparent contradictions within his work.

These philosophers played pivotal roles in shaping Western philosophical thought, and their ideas continue to be studied and debated across academic disciplines. The diversity of their perspectives laid the foundation for the philosophical exploration that followed in subsequent centuries.

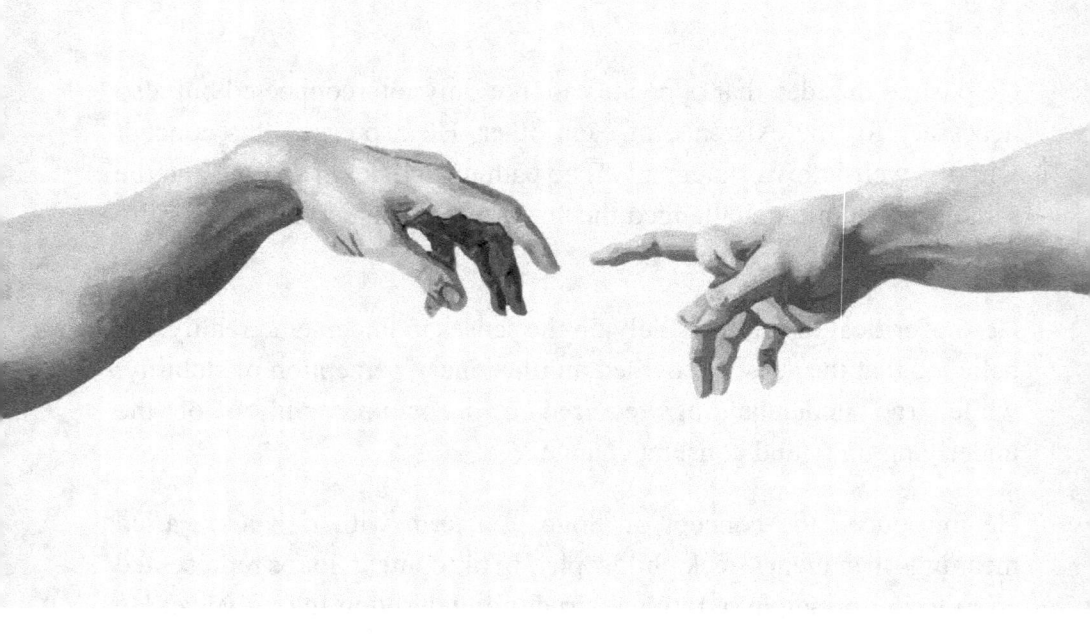

Polymaths: The Renaissance Men

Polymaths are individuals who excel in a wide range of disciplines and fields, showcasing a diverse set of talents and expertise. The Renaissance was a period that particularly celebrated and produced numerous polymaths who made significant contributions to art, science, literature, philosophy, and more.

The Renaissance, a period spanning roughly from the 14th to the 17th century in Europe, marked a profound cultural, artistic, and intellectual rebirth. During this era, individuals who excelled in multiple fields of study and demonstrated a broad range of talents were often referred to as "Renaissance men" or "polymaths." These remarkable individuals played a crucial role in shaping the cultural landscape of their time.

This era of profound cultural, artistic, and intellectual rebirth marked a departure from the constraints of medieval thought. The Renaissance men, with their polymathic pursuits, became the torchbearers of a new age, inspiring generations to come. Their legacy continues to resonate today, reminding us of the enduring power of interdisciplinary exploration and the boundless potential of the human mind.

Leonardo da Vinci:

Leonardo da Vinci was born in 1452 and stands as a quintessential Renaissance polymath, a figure whose multifaceted talents and insatiable curiosity spanned a remarkable array of disciplines. His artistic prowess, evident in masterpieces like the Mona Lisa and The Last Supper, secured his place among the greatest painters in history. Leonardo's works are distinguished by their unparalleled attention to detail, composition, and the innovative use of light and shadow. The Mona Lisa, renowned for its enigmatic smile and subtle sfumato technique, remains an iconic symbol of Renaissance artistry. Similarly, The Last Supper is revered for its emotional depth, dramatic composition, and meticulous depiction of human expression.

Yet, da Vinci's genius transcended the canvas. His contributions extended far beyond the realm of art, showcasing a Renaissance spirit characterized by the fusion of artistic creativity and scientific inquiry. His notebooks, filled with thousands of pages of sketches, observations, and ideas, reveal a profound scientific mind. Delving into the realms of anatomy, Leonardo conducted dissections of the human body and created meticulously detailed drawings. His anatomical studies, though often limited by the technological constraints of his time, laid the groundwork for advancements in medical knowledge.

His designs for flying machines, war machines, and various mechanical devices reflected an imaginative and innovative approach to problem-solving. His interests in mathematics, architecture, and the natural world further solidified his status as a true Renaissance man. His exploration of mathematical principles influenced his artistic compositions, and his architectural sketches revealed a keen understanding of proportion and design.

Leonardo da Vinci's legacy endures not only through the timeless allure of his artistic creations but also through the pioneering spirit that characterized his scientific inquiries and inventive designs. His ability to seamlessly intertwine the worlds of art and science exemplifies the Renaissance ideal of the well-rounded individual, leaving an indelible mark on the cultural and intellectual landscape of his era and beyond.

Michelangelo Buonarroti:

Michelangelo Buonarroti was born in 1475 and emerged as one of the preeminent artistic figures of the Renaissance, leaving an indelible mark on the worlds of sculpture, painting, and architecture.

As a sculptor, Michelangelo's prowess is exemplified in his monumental work, the Statue of David. Carved from a single block of marble, this iconic sculpture captures the biblical hero in a moment of contemplative strength, showcasing Michelangelo's ability to breathe life into stone. The Statue of David, with its harmonious proportions and dynamic pose, is a testament to the artist's skill in conveying both physical and emotional vitality.

In the realm of painting, Michelangelo undertook one of the most ambitious projects of his time—the frescoes of the Sistine Chapel ceiling in the Vatican. The expansive composition features biblical scenes, including the creation of Adam and the Last Judgment, rendered with breathtaking complexity and skill. Painted over four years, the frescoes showcase Michelangelo's mastery of anatomy, composition, and perspective, creating a visual spectacle that remains a pinnacle of Renaissance art.

His architectural legacy is perhaps best represented by his work on St. Peter's Basilica in Rome. While he is often celebrated for his achievements in sculpture and painting, his architectural contributions were significant. He took charge of the project in the mid-16th century, overseeing the completion of the dome, a feat that further solidified the grandeur and magnificence of the basilica. His design principles, rooted in classical aesthetics, emphasized harmony, proportion, and a sense of grandeur, epitomizing the Renaissance ideals of beauty and symmetry.

Like his contemporary Leonardo da Vinci, Michelangelo had a keen interest in anatomy. He conducted dissections of cadavers to deepen his understanding of the human body, particularly muscles and skeletal structures. His anatomical studies, although not as extensive as Leonardo's, demonstrated his commitment to achieving anatomical accuracy in his artistic representations.

He applied his artistic ingenuity to military engineering during times of political unrest in Italy. He was tasked with fortifying the city of Florence, and his strategic designs for fortifications demonstrated his practical understanding of defense structures.

His poetry, written in Italian, Latin, and sometimes even Greek, often reflected his deep introspection, spiritual contemplation, and themes of love and beauty. His verses provided insights into his inner thoughts and philosophical musings.

Michelangelo's lasting impact on the realms of sculpture, painting, and architecture cements his place as one of the giants of Renaissance art.

Galileo Galilei:

Galileo Galilei was born in 1564 and was a prominent figure in the Scientific Revolution, making profound contributions to astronomy, physics, engineering, and mathematics. His work laid the foundation for the scientific method and challenged prevailing views of the cosmos, ushering in a new era of empirical inquiry.

Galileo Galilei's use of the telescope in 1609 marked a revolutionary moment in the history of astronomy, providing a groundbreaking tool for observing celestial bodies and challenging existing cosmological paradigms. Galileo's telescopic observations of the Moon revealed a complex, cratered surface, contradicting the traditional belief in a perfectly smooth and unblemished lunar sphere. His sketches and descriptions documented the existence of mountains and craters, challenging the prevailing Aristotelian notion of celestial perfection.

Galileo's observations provided strong evidence in support of the heliocentric model. The heliocentric model suggested that the Earth and other planets revolved around the Sun, challenging the geocentric model that placed the Earth at the center of the universe. Galileo's findings were instrumental in advancing the heliocentric theory and challenging the long-held Ptolemaic system. Galileo's scrutiny of Venus provided compelling evidence against the geocentric model.

Galileo's most significant discovery through his telescope was the detection of four moons orbiting Jupiter. These satellites—Io, Europa, Ganymede, and Callisto—came to be known as the Galilean moons. While Galileo did observe the rings of Saturn, his telescope's resolution was not sufficient to discern their true nature. At the time, he described them as "ears" or appendages on either side of Saturn. He observed sunspots on the surface of the Sun. His documentation of these dark spots moving across the solar disk provided evidence that the Sun was not a perfect, unchanging celestial body, further challenging traditional Aristotelian cosmology.

In 1632, he published his seminal work, "Dialogue Concerning the Two Chief World Systems," where he presented arguments for the heliocentric model. This work sparked controversy and led to his eventual condemnation by the Catholic Church, which supported the geocentric view. His advocacy for the heliocentric model marked a pivotal moment in the history of the conflict between science and religious orthodoxy.

He formulated the law of falling bodies, demonstrating that all objects, regardless of their mass, fall at the same rate in the absence of air resistance. His experiments on inclined planes and rolling balls contributed to the understanding of motion and acceleration, laying the groundwork for Isaac Newton's laws of motion.

He is often credited with helping to establish the scientific method, a systematic approach to observation, hypothesis formation, experimentation, and the formulation of theories based on empirical evidence. This methodology became a cornerstone of modern scientific practice.

Niccolò Machiavelli:

Niccolò Machiavelli was born in 1469 and was an Italian Renaissance political philosopher, historian, and diplomat. His most famous work, "The Prince" (Il Principe), published in 1532, remains a landmark in political literature, offering pragmatic insights into the acquisition, maintenance, and exercise of political power. Machiavelli's ideas, often characterized by realism and a departure from idealistic notions of leadership, have sparked extensive debate and analysis throughout the centuries.

"The Prince" is a treatise on political power, leadership, and statecraft. It is addressed to Lorenzo de' Medici, seeking to provide practical advice on governance. Unlike previous political writings, this work focuses on the ruthless realities of power politics rather than moral or ethical considerations. He explores the nature of power, the dynamics of leadership, and the strategies that rulers should employ to maintain control.

He argued that political leaders must be willing to set aside conventional moral and ethical standards to secure and maintain power. The famous phrase "the ends justify the means" is often attributed to Machiavelli, encapsulating his pragmatic view. He advocates for leaders to be both loved and feared, but if a choice must be made, it is more prudent to be feared, as fear ensures obedience. Witnessing the rise and fall of various city-states and the interference of foreign powers, he drew from historical examples to illustrate his points.

Machiavelli's work has had a lasting impact on political theory and practice. While some view him as a realist, providing essential insights into the harsh realities of political life, others criticize him for endorsing unethical behavior. Regardless, "The Prince" remains a foundational text that continues to be studied and debated in political science and philosophy.

Nicolaus Copernicus:

Nicolaus Copernicus was born in 1473–1543 and was a Renaissance mathematician and astronomer. His work laid the foundation for the heliocentric model of the solar system, challenging the long-standing geocentric view. His revolutionary ideas, as presented in his major work "De revolutionibus orbium coelestium" ("On the Revolutions of the Celestial Spheres"), marked a turning point in the history of astronomy and had a profound impact on the scientific revolution.

He proposed a heliocentric model in which the Sun, not the Earth, was at the center of the solar system. This was a radical departure from the geocentric model, which had been the prevailing cosmological view for centuries. In his model, the Earth and other planets orbited the Sun, offering a more accurate explanation of the observed movements of celestial bodies.

He retained the use of epicycles (smaller circles within the larger orbits) to account for the observed retrograde motion of planets. However, his model was more elegant and accurate than the complicated systems proposed by earlier astronomers. His book marked a significant departure from the traditional Ptolemaic system, challenging established views and setting the stage for a paradigm shift in scientific thought.

His motivations for proposing the heliocentric model were not only scientific but also driven by a desire for simplicity and elegance in explaining the movements of celestial bodies. However, he was aware of the potential controversy his ideas might provoke, and the publication of his work was somewhat cautious. The heliocentric model faced resistance from both religious and scientific communities initially.

His ideas influenced later astronomers such as Johannes Kepler and Galileo Galilei, who further refined and validated the heliocentric model. The acceptance of Copernican heliocentrism marked a crucial step in the scientific revolution that reshaped the understanding of the natural world. His courageous departure from established views set the stage for a new era of scientific inquiry, where observation, mathematics, and evidence became central to understanding the natural world.

Changing World History

It's essential to note that changing the history of the world does not necessarily require an individual to hold a position of power or fame. Ordinary people can also contribute to historical change through collective actions, grassroots movements, and everyday acts that collectively shift societal attitudes and structures. Ultimately, changing world history involves leaving a lasting impact that shapes the way people think, live, and interact with one another across generations.

The historical landscape is vast and multifaceted, and individuals who left an indelible mark did so through diverse means and in various contexts. Political leaders, philosophers, scientists, and social reformers, among others, have each played pivotal roles, but the weight assigned to their impact often varies based on cultural, geographical, or ideological perspectives.

While some individuals have changed the world through groundbreaking advancements and progressive movements, others have left a lasting imprint through conquests, wars, or the propagation of controversial ideologies. The moral or ethical dimension of their actions becomes a crucial aspect of evaluating their historical significance.

Alexander the Great:

Alexander the Great's impact on the ancient world stands as a testament to the unparalleled scope of his vision, military prowess, and the enduring legacy he left in his wake. Born in 356 BCE, he ascended to the throne of Macedon at a young age, inheriting the mantle of leadership from his father, King Philip II.

From the brilliant tactics employed at the Battle of Issus to the tenacity displayed during the siege of Tyre, each campaign showcased his strategic brilliance and leadership acumen. His army was known for its diversity and disciplined structure.

Alexander's conquests were not solely military; they were also a vehicle for the dissemination of ideas. The blending of Greek philosophy with Eastern wisdom catalyzed a cross-cultural exchange that profoundly shaped the intellectual landscape of the time. The famous meeting with the Indian philosopher Calanus and his inclusion of Persian nobles in his administration underscored his commitment to fostering a cosmopolitan empire.

The legacy of Alexander's conquests endured long after his untimely death in 323 BCE. His empire fragmented into successor states, collectively known as the Diadochi, each continuing to influence the regions they controlled. The Seleucid Empire, Ptolemaic Egypt, and the Hellenistic kingdoms became conduits for the transmission of Greek culture, philosophy, and science, fostering an intellectual renaissance.

Genghis Khan:

Genghis Khan, born around 1162, emerged as a transformative figure in world history, forging the Mongol Empire into a colossal force that spanned continents. His military brilliance, strategic vision, and administrative innovations not only facilitated conquest but also established a system that promoted cultural exchange and economic prosperity.

The Mongol Empire, under his leadership and that of his descendants, evolved into the largest contiguous empire ever known, linking the East and West through the Silk Road. This expansive network of trade and communication facilitated the exchange of goods, ideas, and technologies, fostering a vibrant cross-cultural milieu.

The Pax Mongolica, a period of relative stability and peace, allowed for unprecedented interactions between diverse civilizations, from China to Europe. Genghis Khan's enduring legacy lies not only in the expanse of territory he conquered but also in the enduring impact of the Mongol Empire on the interconnected history of Eurasia.

Martin Luther King Jr.:

Martin Luther King Jr was born on 15th January 1929 in Atlanta, Georgia. His services to humanity transcended the pulpit, extending into transformative actions that reshaped the American landscape. King's leadership during the Civil Rights Movement was marked by nonviolent resistance, challenging systemic racism and advocating for equal rights for African Americans.

His indelible mark is evident in the Montgomery Bus Boycott, the March on Washington, and the pivotal role he played in the passage of the Civil Rights Act of 1964 and the Voting Rights Act of 1965. King's services extended beyond legal victories; they inspired a global movement for justice, equality, and human dignity.

His enduring legacy lies not only in legislative achievements but also in the ongoing struggle for social justice. The Martin Luther King Jr. Day of Service, observed annually, encourages individuals to engage in community projects that embody King's spirit, fostering a society built on the principles of love, equality, and service to others.

Epilogue

The biographies penned in the preceding chapters have not merely chronicled the deeds of historical figures but have sought to unravel the intricacies of the human spirit—the indomitable force that propels individuals to transcend their circumstances and shape the course of history. In recounting the lives of these luminaries, we have journeyed through epochs marked by triumphs and tribulations, revolutions and revelations. These historical figures, once relegated to the records of time, have been resurrected through the written word, their voices echoing across centuries to resonate with our contemporary hearts.

As we reflect upon our own life chapters, we recognize that we are part of an ongoing narrative. The challenges we face and the victories we celebrate are not isolated events but chapters in a saga that began long before us and will continue long after. In this realization, we discover a profound sense of belonging, understanding that our stories are but a continuation of the grand narrative of humanity.

In the echoes of history, we find not only a reflection of the past but a roadmap for the future. The struggles endured, and the victories achieved by these historical figures serve as beacons, illuminating the path ahead for those who dare to dream and strive for a better world.

The flame of ancestral motivation is not an abstract concept; it's the warmth we feel when we connect with our roots. So, as we turn the page to the next chapter, let us carry forward not just the torch of progress but the stories, the laughter, and the lessons learned from our ancestors. Let their humanity be a guiding light, illuminating the path ahead with the wisdom of shared experiences and the enduring strength found in the bonds of family and heritage. In doing so, we not only honor our ancestors but embrace our shared humanity, recognizing that the tapestry of our lives is intricately woven with the threads of countless others who walked this path before us.

For in our pursuit of dreams, in our relentless drive for progress, we pay homage to the silent architects of our existence — our ancestors.

www.ingramcontent.com/pod-product-compliance
Lightning Source LLC
Chambersburg PA
CBHW052201110526
44591CB00012B/2038